RED FIRE
BRANDING

CREATE A
HOT
PERSONAL BRAND
AND HAVE
CUSTOMERS
FOR LIFE

Liz Goodgold

Published by

Happy About

20660 Stevens Creek Blvd., Suite 210 Cupertino, CA 95014

Paperback Edition: September 2011
Hardcover Edition: March 2010
Paperback ISBN: 978-1-60005-204-0 (1-60005-204-5)
Hardcover ISBN: 978-1-60005-173-9 (1-60005-173-1)
Place of Publication: Silicon Valley, California, USA
Library of Congress Number: 2010923583
eBook ISBN: 978-1-60005-174-6 (1-60005-174-X)

Trademarks

Warning and Disclaimer

Look forward
to a sizzling!
Partnership!
Liz

To my son Adam,
Always

Table of Contents

Chapter 1
Light Your Fire:
Understanding Your HOT Personal Brand

Chapter 2
Star Power:
Why You Should Brand Like a Celebrity

Chapter 3
Name Dropping
How to Build a Brand That Sizzles

Chapter 4
Fire Starters:
Understanding the Basics of Intellectual Property

Chapter 9
Dress for Success

Chapter 10
Spice Up the Silence:
Using Music and Voice as Mnemonic Devices

Chapter 11
Feel the Heat:
Using All Senses to Trigger Recall

Chapter 15
Brand Building:
How to Keep the Flame Alive and Avoid Burnout

Chapter 16
Fan the Flames:
Branding Big on a Small Budget 191

Chapter 17
Spread the Fire
How to Use E-mail to Extend Your Brand 201

Preface

Personal Branding for Survival and Success

The invisible secret to success in business today is your personal brand; you need people to remember you in order to do business with you. This book, written with wit and wisdom, shows you how to develop your own personal brand in order to create an indelible image. Then, in step-by-step fashion, you learn practical and tactical techniques to consistently project your brand from your name to music to phrases to developing a signature style. Virtually every point is punctuated with examples from rock stars, sports heroes, TV personalities, famous chefs, business experts, successful entrepreneurs and newsmakers. Develop a strong brand and you reap the recognition, respect, and rewards throughout your entire career.

Learning by Example: Thousands of Real People and Companies

Having had the pleasure of speaking to thousands of audience members in my career, it's become clear to me that we remember stories and examples better than concepts . No matter how many times a professor tries to teach a complicated concept, the light bulb in our heads doesn't turn on until we understand the example. So, stay tuned for page after page of examples from rock stars to celebrities. I'm not saying we should act like a celebrity (red carpet, please!), but that we can become a star in our own field by taking a page from their stage notes.

Red Hot Examples Just Like You

I've met many rising stars in my career and I've taken the liberty of talking about them here. By understanding how a business executive, real estate agent, hairstylist, massage therapist, or saleswoman has adapted a personal branding technique to fit her style, you'll begin to figure out how you can make personal branding work for you. At least, two Red Hot Examples are highlighted in boxes in every chapter.

Battle-Tested and Bullet-Test Strategies

The recommendations, strategies, and tactics suggested in these pages work because they've been market-tested. I am not simply a speaker, but also a marketer who has worked with big brands such as Quaker Oats, Times Mirror, Macmillan Publishing, and Univision. Throughout Red Fire Branding, I translate the core strategies from these big companies into bite-size tactics appropriate for small businesses.

Quick, Easy-to-Read for Today's A.D.D. Lifestyle

As I believe that everyone today is afflicted with ADD (Attention Deficit Disorder), quick bursts of information are better than long, draw-out explanations. Look inside this book to see Words of Lizdom, Strike the Match exercises (just like Mix N' Match from your grade school classroom), and Your Turn to Act where you can turn your reading into action.. If you're in a hurry (aren't we all?) just skim through these boxes and you'll get the gist of the chapter. It's just like Cliff Notes - only better. This format allows you to jump from chapter to chapter and still master its key branding concepts.

Exercises to Put Learning Into Action

Since this book was written as a hands-on book, every chapter concludes with hands-on exercises entitled Your Turn to Act. These are your homework, your "to do" list, the step-by-step formula for creating your own, strong, personal brand. I recommend that you create a Council of Advisers: colleagues, clients, investors, or even family members to help you get an outsider perspective. You'll see the Council referred to often in your exercises to act as a reality check.

May all your dreams come true and may your business grow like wild fire. I welcome your comments.

Liz Goodgold

Liz@redfirebranding.com

Chapter 1

Light Your Fire:
Understanding Your HOT Personal Brand

STRIKE THE MATCH

Pair the correct attribute with the brand name that made it famous:

FAMOUS ATTRIBUTE		BRAND NAME
1. Queen of Reinventing Herself	A	Sandra Bullock
2. Girl Next Door	B	Tina Turner
3. Outrageous Outfits	C	Queen Latifah
4. Ditsy Blonde	D	Dolly Parton
5. Model-Perfect Prisoner	E	Mark Spitz
6. Germ Phobic Game Show Host	F	Madonna
7. Killer Legs	G	Matthew McConaughey
8. Belly-Dancer Hips	H	Eve
9. Famous Booty	I	Cher
10. Bodacious Bosom	J	Lauren Hutton
11. Tiger Paw Tattoo	K	Goldie Hawn
12. '70s Moustache	L	Naomi Campbell
13. Full-Figured Gal	M	Howie Mandel
14. Gap-Toothed Model	N	Shakira
15. 6-Pack Abs	O	Jennifer Lopez

This Hot Book Is for You

This book was written to help you—entrepreneurs, consultants, new business owners, therapists, real estate agents, and multi-level marketers—to spark sales by branding yourself so you can stand out from the sea of similarity.

In today's cluttered, competitive world, you must create an indelible image that sizzles in order to be remembered and rewarded. Self-promotion is a non-stop, full-time job. It is not vanity—it is survival! And, in a down economy, it is the folks who are recognized by their peers and prospects who will get rewarded. Branding is your visibility; it is your way to stay "on fire" instead of "getting fired."

If you are a real estate agent, hair stylist, massage therapist, or esthetician, then this book will teach you how to become your own talking, walking mascot. It will teach you how to ensure that you are the brand customers follow wherever you may work.

If you are a lawyer, accountant, or other business professional, then this book will help you light a fire under your business in appropriate ways without advertising.

If you represent Arbonne, Avon, Usana, Silpada, Tupperware, Mary Kay, Send Out Cards, Cookie Lee Jewelry, or any other multi-level marketing line, then this book will ignite your sales by showing you how to recruit other distributors, build your customer base, and retain current customers.

If you are a new business owner who is an expert, but not in marketing, then this book will act as kindling—fueling the flames to build an entire marketing plan.

If you're thinking about starting a business, then this book will arm you with the creative foundation you need to start analyzing the marketplace and positioning yourself as an expert.

And, if you are a C-level executive charged with growing the business, then this book will fuel innovative thinking by providing abundant examples of how other companies are successfully implementing innovative branding techniques.

The Time Is *Now!*

This is your time. This is your moment! Seize it! Here is your chance to fuel the flames not only of positive thinking, but also of positive doing! This is your chance to create a strong brand that will fire you up to achieve your goals. It's time to stop waiting and watching. It's time to start doing!

WORDS of "*LIZ*DOM"

PERFECTION DELAYED

As you start working your way through the action steps in this book, remember to just start doing; don't think that it has to be perfect, since sometimes "done is better than perfect."

Welcome to Branding!

Branding is fun, hot, and creative. It is not difficult, it is not complicated, and you can do it! Even with a quick thumb-through of this book, you'll notice that there aren't any illegible graphs, pie charts, or even spread sheets. Why? Because I believe branding is logical. I believe that once you grasp the key concepts, you'll smack your hand on your forehead and exclaim, "I get it!"

Most importantly, branding is the secret weapon for keeping your customers for life. All of the ideas, tactics, and recommendations in this book are to ensure that you remain top of mind with your current customers: if they continue to remember you, they continue to do business with you. In branding, out of sight is not just out of mind—it's out of business.

WORDS of "*LIZ*DOM"

DEFINITION OF BRANDING

Branding is how others perceive you based upon every single interaction you have with them; it's not only your planned marketing messages, such as Web sites, business cards, logos, or advertising, but it's also the unofficial messages communicated through phone calls, e-mail messages, blog postings, articles, and personal interaction.

Branding Is about Perception

Let's start by talking about what branding is not: it isn't a hot iron searing into your hide (although with the proliferation of outrageous tattoos, that might someday be true). And it isn't your logo, Web site, TV commercial, or slogan. It is, rather, the sum total of all of these marketing messages, including unintended ones delivered via blogs, e-mail messages, social networking, and voice mail greetings that influence how others see you.

Aha! Your brand is not what you say it is. It's what others say it is.

You might walk around like William Hung believing you are destined to be a rock star on American Idol (remember "She Bangs"?), but in reality you can't carry a tune. In fact, Hung became famous not because he can sing, but because he can't!

WORDS of "*LIZ*DOM"

THE SIMON COWELL EFFECT

Sometimes you need to face a fierce reality check about your talents, goals, and dreams. Test your skills in front of a Simon-type arbiter to determine if, honestly, you have the requisite skill to be a star in your field.

Remember that perception can be stronger than reality. From my days of working at Quaker Oats, I can tell you that Old Fashioned Oats are the best-selling brand in the grocery store. But in blind taste tests, I guarantee you that most shoppers cannot find one single difference between private-label oats and the branded ones. Ford Motor Company is also tackling perception, but in the opposite direction. Some car buyers today don't even put this American company onto their short list of consideration. The perception lingers that Ford cars are unreliable, gas guzzlers, and more appropriate for a previous generation.

Your Brand Must Be Authentic

As you start to discover, identify, and project your brand, it's critical to present a true representation of you. A very cool, hip image is meaningless if you're still trying to figure out how to text message, create a Facebook page, or recommend someone on LinkedIn.

On the other hand, if you're known for being a conservative expert, then prim and proper suits, formal language, and exacting precision are perfect components for blazing a trail for your brand.

Adapting Corporate Branding Ideas to Personal Brands

I often hear from my audiences that branding is expensive and that it is reserved for big companies like Nike, United Airlines, and Coca-Cola, with even bigger budgets. But the truth is that branding principles taken from consumer product companies and applied to the brand called "you" can bring enormous benefits. OK, let's take Southwest Airlines and see how we can identify a few of its branding traits. Then, we can figure out how to adapt them to fit a personal brand.

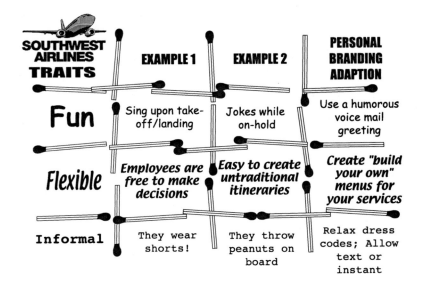

SOUTHWEST AIRLINES TRAITS	EXAMPLE 1	EXAMPLE 2	PERSONAL BRANDING ADAPTION
Fun	Sing upon take-off/landing	Jokes while on-hold	Use a humorous voice mail greeting
Flexible	*Employees are free to make decisions*	*Easy to create untraditional itineraries*	*Create "build your own" menus for your services*
Informal	They wear shorts!	They throw peanuts on board	Relax dress codes; Allow text or instant

So you can see that we actually can learn lessons from the big boys. In fact, the purpose of this entire book is to have you practicing an inordinate amount of R and D: Rip-off and Duplicate. I want you to look at great branding ideas and adapt them to fit you.

Brands Stand for One Thing

Of course, to build your brand, you'll need to determine what your brand is. What do I mean by that? I mean you have to find out what you stand for. Of course, many of you might already know that you stand for quality products, good customer services, great prices, and value. I would argue that every business today must at least possess those qualities. A great brand goes beyond core competencies to unearth special personality traits and promises that are inextricably linked to the brand. Consistency and creativity is king.

BILLIE JEAN KING

Billie Jean King has truly earned her place as a "brand." Consider these milestones: thirty-nine Grand Slam Titles; the first female commissioner in sports history; the first woman to ever have a sports venue named after her (The Billie Jean King National Tennis Center); and the first female tennis player to earn $100,000 in a single sports season.

Today, it's easy to forget the amazing barriers that Billie Jean King broke in her long career of fighting for equal pay for women on the tennis circuit. Her relentless efforts against sexism culminated in the historic "battle of the sexes" match and her victory over former Wimbledon champ Bobby Riggs in 1973, stunning and silencing her critics. Her greatest accomplishment was the inspiration she gave so many women: the courage to follow and fulfill their dreams—not only in tennis, but also in business and in life. I certainly admire and thank her for that!

Create a Council

Before you can implement any of the branding techniques highlighted in this book, you must be clear on your brand and its point of difference. I recommend creating a Council of Advisers, using a Mastermind Group, enlisting your Vistage colleagues, or asking your Board of Directors for assistance. This group should help answer your burning questions and act as your reality test. It should be such a strong group that its members are not afraid to tell you if your idea is sure to quickly go down in flames. (Or, as I like to say, "Sometimes the baby really is ugly!")

At the end of this chapter and every chapter, you'll see "Your Turn to Act," a series of action steps that will help you start, define, and strengthen your brand. Your Council can play an important role throughout these exercises.

Create a Niche

I used to hear that Volvo stands for safety (such a tired 1999 example). As we move into the twenty-first century, we can see that brands evolve and that Volvo no longer stands for safety. In reality, Volvo now stands for your parent's car and you don't want to drive one!

Howard Schultz's goal was for Starbucks to stand for the experience—the destination between home and work where you could linger, read, or catch up with your BFF (Best Friend Forever). Today, that vision is blurry as Starbucks faces plummeting sales, a struggling economy, and numerous new product missteps.

Perhaps a chart of today's brands might look as follows:

BRAND	WHAT IT STANDS FOR
(Apple)	*Hot, up-to-the-minute electronics*
LEXUS	*THE luxury car of the twenty-first century*
WHOLE FOODS MARKET	*Delicious, expensive good-for-you food*
MANOLO BLAHNIK	*Killer, hip, high heels*
twitter	*THE high-tech way to keep in touch with friends*

Do you see the trend? Great brands stand for one thing; there is not a laundry list here of all of the qualities of an I-Pod or of Twitter. Instead, there's a shorthand label of the one key perception of the brand.

WORDS of "*LIZ*DOM"

SPECIALIZATION IS THE KEY

Great brands are specialized; they stand for one thing only. To brand successfully, you cannot be all things to all people.

SUDS

Therefore, I am asking you to specialize. I'm asking you to pick, promote, project, and publicize the one thing that you do better and differently than anyone else. Dr. Mary Beth McCabe, of Sun Marketing, founded her business with this niche: Hispanic advertising and media buying. For over fifteen years, she has earned her reputation as the "go to" woman after implementing successful sales campaigns to the influential Hispanic population for companies as diverse as Gerber Foods and local car dealerships.

Mark Amtower specializes in a very unique area: business-to-government marketing. His niche is so narrow that he easily got a radio gig on the only Washington DC-based station that focuses on the federal government! His site is branded as Federal Direct and is loaded with so much information that one can easily see him as the expert in this area.

With specialization, you are looking for a knee-jerk reacti
tion a niche and your name should immediately pop up.
power of specialization this way: it allows you to more easily be recognized
as the expert; it reduces your workload and research time since you're only
keeping up in one area; and most importantly, it allows you to charge a
premium price! If, Heaven forbid, you were diagnosed with cancer, I guarantee that you would not seek out not a general practitioner, but the best
oncologist you could find.

Or, if you're like me and just craving a juicy, fast-food dose of grease, I'm
going to In-N-Out Burger. I only have six menu item choices, but they are
the best choices. All we need at that type of place is a cheeseburger, fries,
a Diet Coke (don't ask me why!), and perhaps a malt. Done! The power of
specialization!

Essentials of a Strong Brand Positioning

To create a hot brand, you must start with these critical four components:

1. **A clearly defined target**—You're not trying to appeal to all
   buyers, just those with specific characteristics based upon
   their demographics (age, sex, income), price sensitivity,
   behavior, and even psychographics. The term psychographics is merely a fancy word for categorizing people by
   their mindset. Gatorade, for example, targets exercise-
   minded enthusiasts. (Note: the intended target doesn't
   actually have to exercise, they just have to believe they do.)
   Sean Curtis, with his family-run business Coffee
   Ambassador, targets companies within certain zip codes—
   specifically law firms, accounting firms, real estate companies, and brokerage houses with fifteen or more employees. This clear, narrowly defined target criteria is based
   upon years of learning which types of businesses within
   certain areas and with a minimum number of employees
   are more likely to purchase. In short, targeting lets you
   market, brand, and sell more efficiently.

2. **Frame of reference**—It's important to understand your competition. From the customer's perspective, what are the alternatives to your service? Cloud 9 Shuttle recognizes that it not only competes against Super Shuttle and other shuttle services, but also against any other mode of transportation to the airport, including your brother, sister, and spouse as well as limo services, the train, taxi, or trolley. Therefore, do not make the mistake of only thinking of competitors within your category.

3. **Emotionally based promise**—In order to build a strong brand, you must have a strong emotional connection. People must care about you, your service, or your product. In other words, indifference is the antithesis of branding. Your goal is to create such a difference that people will choose you over your competitors. It is as if they will specify Coke over Pepsi, Nike over Adidas, or Dell over Hewlett-Packard. To continue with the Gatorade example, the company promises that this drink hydrates customers so well that they can accomplish overwhelmingly great feats such as those by Michael Jordan or Tiger Woods.

4. **Fact-based support for point of difference**—Brands today cannot survive just upon platitudes. What are the facts, systems, and documentation to support your promises and point of difference? Gatorade backs up its promise with solid scientific research and even has its own lab where the company is constantly testing performance. Testimonials and case studies work well here to show results.

Example of a Strongly Positioned Brand: Federal Express:

- **TARGET**: Business owners and corporations willing to pay for peace of mind

- **FRAME OF REFERENCE**: Shipping/freight market

- **EMOTIONALLY BASED PROMISE**: When it absolutely, positively has to be there, we guarantee it.

- **PRODUCT-BASED SUPPORT**: State-of-the art scanning and tracking system, continuous package innovation (Tyvek, Overnight Letter, etc.)

If Your Services All Don't Fit into One Brand: Invent a New One!

If you're sitting there wondering how you're ever going to narrow down all of your great services into one strong brand, I've got a secret strategy for you: invent a new brand.

MANNY OTERO

Manny Otero started InSane Diego Productions, a mobile DJ company, on April 1, 2003 (no joke!). Initially, his company focused on fun, corporate events, but brides began calling as well. Soon, Manny added brides to his target list, but he found that although the prospect calls were increasing, he wasn't closing the same percentage of business that he was with corporate.

By talking to prospects and customers, he discovered that since brides don't have the same needs, questions, and expectation as a business prospect, his current brand name and marketing materials weren't resonating. In 2007, he created a new brand called Memories and Music Entertainment. With this brand, he's captured the ethereal quality of a wedding as well as the heartstrings and purse strings of the engaged. Oh, and his wedding business is up over 20 percent since the creation of the separate brand. Hot idea!

Great brands have used the birth of a second brand as a successful spin-off for decades. It works when the product, intended target, point of different, or price point is very different than the original brand. Here are some time-tested examples.

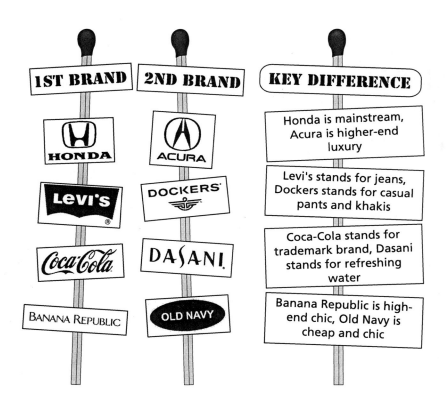

1ST BRAND	2ND BRAND	KEY DIFFERENCE
HONDA	ACURA	Honda is mainstream, Acura is higher-end luxury
Levi's	DOCKERS	Levi's stands for jeans, Dockers stands for casual pants and khakis
Coca-Cola	DASANI	Coca-Cola stands for trademark brand, Dasani stands for refreshing water
BANANA REPUBLIC	OLD NAVY	Banana Republic is high-end chic, Old Navy is cheap and chic

Know What You Are and What You Aren't

A fundamental element of good branding is that it should define what you are and what you are not, what you do and what you don't. Think of yourself as your own walking, talking mascot—perhaps like Tony the Tiger, the Jolly Green Giant, or even the Energizer Bunny. Then, think about which actions are appropriate to that mascot. For example, Grand Met, then the owner of Pillsbury, made a monumental mistake when their sweet and cuddly Doughboy appeared in a bar with rap-type music playing. Oh no!

I often tell prospects that while I do give an entertaining talk, I don't do PowerPoint. It quickly defines me.

WORDS of "*LIZ*DOM"

WHAT YOU ARE AND AREN'T

Good branders routinely tell others what they are and what they aren't—what they do and what they never do.

1. **Your Brand Positioning**—Ask yourself these key questions: What do I want to be known for? What do I do better and different than anyone else? What work do I do that stirs my passion and brings me the most joy?

2. **Test Your Goal Against Reality**—List all of the products and services that you provide. Then, start equating how much revenue actually comes from each component. You might find, for example, that although you perform both audits and taxes, 75 percent of your revenue is truly tax-time work. Ask yourself if this is the niche you want. How does it compare with your goal? Make notes of the difference between where you are and where you want to go.

3. Write your Council an e-mail to provide you with 7-10 adjectives about you. Caring, funny, detail-oriented are all valid terms. Review this list to look for overlapping traits. These adjectives are the beginning of the genus of your brand. Also, pay attention to any blatant conflicts in these personality traits, because such conflicts signal trouble. You may have to play up or down one of those characteristics.

4. Try to find at least three of these traits that you believe ring true. Then, look for ways to talk about these traits, use these traits, and illustrate them in business. For example, if your colleagues consider you to be the King of Follow-Up, make a point in your voice mail to tell callers that you guarantee you will return their phone call within 20 hours. That is walking the walk.

Chapter 2

Star Power:
Why You Should Brand Like a Celebrity

STRIKE THE MATCH

Pair the correct hairstyle with the celebrity that made it famous:

HAIRSTYLE	BRAND NAME
1. Dual Hair Buns	A Yul Brenner
2. Helmet Hair	B Crystal Gayle
3. Extremely Long Hair	C Whoopi Goldberg
4. Twin Long Braids with Bandana	D Princess Leia
5. Dreadlocks	E Willie Nelson
6. Bleached Blonde	F Donald Trump
7. Curly Red Hair	G Dorothy Hamil
8. Bald	H Little Orphan Annie
9. The Wedge	I Marilyn Monroe
10.The Rachel	J Jennifer Aniston

Become a Celebrity in Your Own Field

For better or worse, we live in a celebrity-obsessed world. Stars are often paid enormous fees just to make an appearance, are given free designer merchandise, are flocked by admirers, and are tracked by the traditional and online media. We too can gain celebrity status in our field, but probably without the paparazzi. The celebrity status phenomenon will bring you more prospects, greater name recognition, and the assumption that you are even better qualified than you are!

The Power of Consistency

Trailblazers in the news today have assistants, coaches, stylists, trainers, vocal coaches, and "botoxologists" to ensure that they perennially look, flawless, and dress with equal panache in every public appearance. Our challenge is to adapt these resources to boost our own profiles.

The number-one secret to successful branding is consistency. It builds and meets expectations and keeps your brand burning. I often hear from Americans traveling abroad that they can't wait to hop into a McDonald's and grab a burger. Why? Because they know what they're going to get. In most locales, especially across the United States, the food tastes exactly the same from one location to the next. This consistency is not a fault, but a key attribute.

WORDS of "LIZDOM"

THE GOLDEN RULE OF BRANDING

The secret to great branding is consistency; every appearance and every interaction demands that you project the same image.

SUDS

If celebrities veer from this golden rule of branding, they misfire. When Kerri Russell, then the high school star of Felicity, cut her trademark tumbling mane of curls, viewership fell and never recovered. When Sylvester Stallone tried his hand at comedy (heaven help us!), with *Stop or My Mom Will Shoot*, it backfired. Sly needs to recognize that he only succeeds when he plays the two roles that we expect: Rambo and Rocky.

And, can we please have back our lovely Meg Ryan? After *Sleepless in Seattle, When Harry Met Sally*, and *You've Got Mail*, she endeared us to her movies. But once she decided that she was going to be a "serious" actor, we've had nothing but bombs. Raise your hand if you've seen any of these: *Restoration, The Deal, In the Land of Women*, or *My Mom's New Boyfriend*. They all went straight to video.

Critics have voiced disappointment with Katie Couric's "performance" on the CBS news, but that's not accurate. It's not that she's a bad anchor; it's that our image of her as the perky, happy co-host is inconsistent with her hard-hitting news about murders, bombings, and terrorists.

Behavior Must Meet Expectations

When expectations and realities clash, you have the makings of a disaster. Witness Mel Gibson. His anti-Semitic remarks were major news because we didn't expect this type of behavior. Tiger Woods, known for his grace under pressure, projected the exact opposite image when the debacle of his many affairs became tabloid fodder. Michael Phelps' little episode with inhaling was also newsworthy because we didn't expect it from this "apple-pie"Olympian, and normally steady Tom Cruise's over-the-top jumping on Oprah's couch made us rethink his sanity.

I remember a fellow speaker who appeared to be panicking after a major problem arose. Watching his display of frenetic behavior, I remember asking myself, "Isn't he a specialist in stress management?"

You must walk the walk and talk the talk. Choose your brand image and examine its authenticity carefully.

Pick a Celebrity Brand to Emulate

When defining your own career goals, it's often easier to explain to others by translating the unfamiliar to the familiar. For example, when I worked in publishing, I would state that a new book "is a spy thriller a la Tom Clancy, but set in the 1800s." Or, "it is just like James Bond, but the lead character is a woman."

It might be easier to define your goal as simply "to become the Oprah Winfrey of Parenting" or the "Michael Jordan of Racquetball". It also helps you to determine what worked in their past and what might work for you.

The benefits of celebrity branding are profuse:

> **1: Commands a Premium Price:** We've already hinted at one of the great rewards of branding: commanding a premium price. Look at it this way; that Chanel suit is never going to go on-sale. And, neither is Ermenegildo Zegna's made-to-measure jacket. If you're branded well, prospects

view your higher price as reinforcement of
one of the critical reasons why cutting the
services is a major no-no; it undervalues yo
compels you to compete based on price, w
long-term losing proposition (unless you a

Harrison Ford boasts the highest number of million-dollar
grossing films in history. Is it any wonder that he can command $20 million per film? Or, consider Madonna, who
inked one of the most lucrative contract deals ever with
Live Nation, estimated to be worth $120 million over ten
years.

2: Creates Awareness: If you build a strong brand, people
will know about you even if they can't do business with
you. Over ten years ago, Pfizer introduced Viagra and it
seemed to be the buzz-generator at every level. Did I know
about it? Yes. Was it intended for me? No!

Or, how about Lauren Conrad and her "feud" with fellow
OC star Heidi Montag? I've never seen the show, but her
profile has allowed her the financial backing to launch her
own designer label and appear in an AT&T commercial.
Nothing succeeds like success.

3: Builds Loyalty: The most fiercely loyal consumer today
remains the cigarette smoker. When was the last time you
heard a tried-and-true Marlboro Man say, "let me try the
Kools just for kicks?" No way!

I admit to being a rabid reader, and I routinely devour
books by Steve Martini, Alisa Valdes-Rodriguez, Sheldon
Siegel, and Michael Connelly. I don't even need to see the
reviews. Once the book is published, I can't wait to read it
because I am that loyal.

In 1985, Ken Druck wrote a book entitled *Secrets Men Keep*.
Then, through the tragic death of his daughter Jenna, he
created a foundation to keep her spirit alive while trans-

orming the lives of young women. Since then, he has appeared on Oprah, Larry King Live, and CNN so often that invariably he hears, "do I know you?" Now, just his name opens doors.

4: Generates Word-of-Mouth Buzz: Bonnie Raitt had it right when she sang: "Let's give 'em something to talk about." If you're generating chatter, you're generating interest. And building interest and awareness is the first step to purchase intent.

Phillips Electronics created an outrageous video ad called "shave everywhere" to promote its new razor; it had over 250,000 visitors in its first month! Career Builder created one of my favorite viral campaigns: Monkey E-mails. Over 44 million monkey e-mails were sent after it aired during Super Bowl 2007.

A few outstanding restaurants have mastered this concept. They make sure that they have the best chips, freshest bread, or homemade margaritas. It allows a visitor to succinctly say one positive statement about the place. Bistro 110 in Chicago is famous for its roasted garlic heads to accompany the bread; Bradley Ogden can make me cry with his Bleu Cheese Soufflé; Deborah Scott's Steaks on Fire is a dish not to be missed; and I'll never forget foie gras with orange chocolate sauce at Lutèce.

JUDD LAIPPLY

RED HOT EXAMPLE

You might not know his name, but I bet you've heard, read, or watched "The Evolution of Dance." On YouTube, where his fast-forward imitation of all of the dance crazes from the hustle to the twist is posted, his video has been viewed over 1 million times! He even caught the eye of Oprah, who invited him on her show and further expanded his reach. Thanks to the Web success and word-of-mouth buzz, Judd now commands top dollar for each of his speeches, has thousands in his audience, and always ends his talk with a variation of "the dance." Way to boogie!

5: Increases Referrals: As you can see, having something to say about a person or place allows for easier referrals. Since most small and service businesses rely on the power of referrals, it's essential to build a strong brand to ensure a never-ending supply of them.

WORDS of "*LIZ*DOM"

THE BENEFITS OF BRANDING

The benefits of branding build upon each other, creating an exponential wheel of possibilities and revenue. Each one relies upon the other to propel your business forward.

6: Increases Recognition: We have transformed into a visual society; almost 96 percent of all communication today is visual. Therefore, it's important for others to quickly recognize you whether at a networking event, a trade convention, on the platform, or at your own business meeting.

If Suze Orman walked into your office right now, the odds are good that you'd recognize her, right? In fact, she has built her brand image so well that she's now doing the famous "got milk?" commercials, consulting for Avon sales representatives, and trying to secure a Folgers deal. Not bad, eh?

BETH ANDREWS

RED HOT EXAMPLE

Beth Andrews, at five feet nothin', is a true spitfire. Based in Atlanta, she has spent over twenty years in sales, reaching the top selling spot virtually every year for Macmillan Publishing, Addison-Wesley, and Pearson Publishing. She's not a star in all industries, but only in the highly specialized field of textbook sales, allowing her to become a very big fish in a very small pond. Her trademark blonde hair, Southern accent, and geographically challenged height make her a force to be reckoned with!

7: Increases Credibility: Building a strong personal brand allows you instant credibility. Every positive facet of branding builds upon the other to create increasing awareness and rewards: people read about you, thereby allowing you to command more for your services; they hear about you from one source and then the buzz begins.

The bottom-line is that if people have heard about you, then they believe you are more valuable than your invisible competitor. The noise generated about you through all of your efforts results in more prospects, opportunities, and more customers with less work. Your customer base has been pre-sold.

MONEY SAVING TIP *Sign up your Web site for free Google Analytics at www.google.com/analytics to understand Web visitors, most viewed pages, and other essential metrics.*

It's good to start your branding efforts with a few quantitative baseline measurements. Then, in six months, you can begin to measure the results. Here are a few ways to start:

TEST YOUR WEB PRESENCE; note how many references are on the key search engines such as Google, Yahoo, and Bing.

LOOK AT THE NUMBER of weekly Web visitors to your site.

NOTE how many opt-ins you have for your e-mail list.

COMPILE THE ACTIVITY of your e-mail readers, noting how many times your newsletter was forwarded, how many times a link was clicked, etc.

GET AN AVERAGE of how frequently, if ever, reporters contact you and how often it turns into media placement.

KEEP TRACK of how many referrals you get in one month.

Chapter 3

Name Dropping
How to Build a Brand That Sizzles

Pair the correct birth name with
the new brand created:

NEW BRAND

BIRTH NAME

1. Dana Owens
2. Archibald Leach
3. Caryn Johnson
4. O'Shea Jackson
5. Allen Konigsberg
6. Tara Leigh Patrick
7. Gladys Leeman
8. Ralph Lipschitz
9. Stacy Ferguson
10. Melvin Kaminsky
11. Natasha Nikolaevna Gurdin
12. Joyce Wilhelmina Frankenberg
13. Betty Perske

A Jane Seymour
B Fergie
C Woody Allen
D Queen Latifah
E Mel Brooks
F Kirstie Alley
G Natalie Wood
H Cary Grant
I Whoopi Goldberg
J Carmen Electra
K Lauren Bacall
L Ice Cube
M Ralph Lauren

The New School of Thought: Don't Name the Company after Yourself

All great brands start with a name. The old school of thought was that naming the company after yourself dramatically increased your exposure. **Wrong!** I'm here to acquaint you with the new thinking about branding—naming the company after yourself limits expansion, recruitment efforts, sale of the company, publicity efforts, and even product and service offerings.

Difficult Names Can Lead to Problems

Your name may have negative connotations—Hazard Construction, Mangled Florist, and Grief Financial Services have all failed to recognize that it's tough to do business with a company that appears as if it's sending you down the path of destruction. (Good grief! Did they lose all of my money? Are all of your flowers mangled? Is construction really a hazard?)

Customers Only Want to Deal with You

If your name is the only one on the letterhead, your customers will only want to deal with you. No matter how experienced your staff, the moment a problem emerges or a VIP calls, the phone call gets routed to you. And what happens when you open multiple offices or stores and you can only be at one place at a time? Trust me, irate customers will only want to deal with you, the de facto leader.

Who Wants to Be CEO of You?

Again, if your name is the brand, how do you recruit and retain top talent? How many executives want to be CEO with your name on the door? All of their efforts wrap right around back to you. Furthermore, even with you still in charge, big hitters will often leave as they question your succession planning.

Self-Named Companies Limit Expansion

Sometimes naming the company something like Jane Smith & Associates also limits your expansion; the name sounds small-time even if you've hit the big time. Given the current downsized economy, so many displaced workers have become entrepreneurs by default that a common perception is that you're a temporary consultant until a "real job" comes along.

WORDS of "LIZDOM"

TRADEMARKING A NAME

Just because a name is available for trademark, doesn't mean it's a good name.

SUDS

Self-Named Companies Hinder the Opportunity to Sell Your Company or Start a New One

If you become so successful that eventually buyers for your business knock on your door, watch out! Selling the business with your name on it may prevent you from using your own name again in a similar industry.

Look at the case of Wally Amos, creator of the *Famous Amos* cookie brand. After selling the company initially in 1978, he realized that he still had the appetite to create new products. The minute he introduced a candy, he was hit with a cease and desist order and was prevented by the courts from ever using his name in connection with any item in the confectionery industry. Ouch! He eventually became so disgruntled that he named his new company *Uncle NoName.*

More recently, Joseph Abboud was sued by JA Apparel for using his own name in connection with the brand. The short story is that the famous designer sold his company, including his brand name, for $65 million. When he launched a new company called "jaz" after his non-compete period ended all was fine. But, his tagline is "a new composition by designer Joseph Abboud" fueled out cries of misappropriating the trademark that he no longer owns. The suit has not yet been settled, but I'd be betting that the designer loses this round.

Selling Your Business Means Someone Else Manages It

What happens if your self-named company is purchased, but you now no longer like the product or its advertising? It's still your name on the package. The Freeman clan wants its hair care and beauty line back from Dial Corporation. "I was watching Dial destroy what it took me twenty-five years to build," says Larry Freeman, founder of Freeman Cosmetics. And look at Vidal Sassoon, who is struggling with Procter & Gamble to get his brand back and manage it himself.

First Names Are Difficult to Protect

Often, using just your first name can also be hazardous to your business success. With a generic name, like Bill's Diner for example, it's hard to be the only one in the country. Oscar's, a San Diego-based pizza chain that was acquired by Sizzler Corporation, had no choice but to change its name in 2001. Why? Hilton Hotels Corporation not only owns the trademark to the name Oscar's, but also operates four restaurants under that brand in New York City and overseas. Of course, the publicity materials quote Oscar Sarkisian as stating that he is honoring his wife for all of her hard work and has now changed the name to *Pat & Oscars*. Really?

Your Personal Actions Impact the Company Image

When Steve Madden was sentenced to over three years in jail in 2002 for securities fraud and money laundering, investors were leery. Part of his sentence barred him for seven years from serving as an officer or director of any public company, including his own fashion-forward *Steven Madden Ltd. Company*. Although the company has had mixed results mostly due to poorly forecasted fashion trends, the company's fate is far from secure.

Look at the recent case of Martha Stewart, the doyenne of homemaking. Although her company and its stock hemorrhaged red ink while she was in jail and the stock price fell 40 percent in 2001, today she has proven to be as strong as *Teflon*. She has new alliances with *KB Home, Singer Sewing Machines, Macy's,* and of course, her long-standing partnership with *Kmart.* But, not all of us can come out of jail smelling like freshly baked bread.

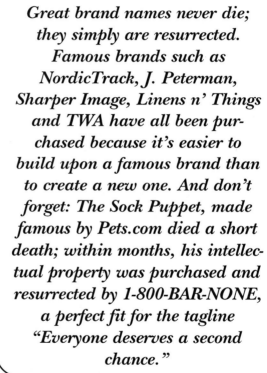

WORDS of "*LIZ*DOM"

GREAT BRANDS NEVER DIE

Great brand names never die; they simply are resurrected. Famous brands such as NordicTrack, J. Peterman, Sharper Image, Linens n' Things and TWA have all been purchased because it's easier to build upon a famous brand than to create a new one. And don't forget: The Sock Puppet, made famous by Pets.com died a short death; within months, his intellectual property was purchased and resurrected by 1-800-BAR-NONE, a perfect fit for the tagline "Everyone deserves a second chance."

SUDS

So, if we now know how not to name, this is the time to arm you with the arsenal necessary to help you judge a good name. Whether you create your own name or hire a naming consultant, it's essential that you understand these criteria.

The Seven Criteria Necessary to Create a Good Name

1. Be Positive: Sounds pretty obvious, doesn't it? Yet, why would there exist brand names such as *Loóza*? Or *Country Clutter*? Or *Step Back*? Or *Danger*? I dislike the weight scale called *Upscale*, because I'm always trying to get my weight down, not up! Yes, all of these product names and company names exist, even though they have negative connotations.

2. Marry the Selling Proposition to the Name: A good name that actually promotes the benefits of your brand can be enormously successful. Think of *Sunkist*, or *Duracell*, or *Renuzit*, or *Rentokil*, or even the *Roach Motel*. At the same time, compare these to the confusingly titled *Gentleman's Quarter*, where most of its revenue is derived from the sale of women's clothes!

3. Pleasant Sounding: Most of the time, a brand will be spoken aloud rather than read. After all, aren't we all looking for that elusive word-of-mouth referral? Mellifluous names can be a pleasure to say. Compare how beautiful the brand name *Caress* sounds versus *Dial*, or compare *Wawanesa* to *Unum*. Note that in America, we tend to have an enormous bias against the "u" sound. Look at words like Regus, Muth, and Indus. For some reason, we just don't like them. Maybe it's because they sound like swear words.

Ask your kids for their favorite food words and you might get back these humdingers as I did: moo goo gai pan, ratatouille (before the movie), frittata, and couscous. These words are all fun to say because some of them are duplicated sounds (tutu, Coca-Cola, Bora Bora, etc.) Feel free to let the word "reduplicated" roll off your tongue and impress your friends at the next dinner party!

WORDS of "*LIZ*DOM"

FULL FRONTAL NAMING

Sometimes creating a "Full Frontal" name will work—what you see is what you get. Think of Avon's "Skin-So-Soft" or "I Can't Believe it's Not Butter" as examples.

SUDS

4. Easy to Say: Not only do we want words that sound good, but we also want words that are easy to say. It's a fine line between foreign words that have caché and words that are completely unpronounceable. *Prego, Tazo,* and *Pronto* have more easily moved into our vocabulary than brands such as *Akamai*, and *Touareg*. I have yet to be able to correctly request make-up at the *Lancôme* counter because I can't say, "Absolue Rouge" or "Maquicontrôl". In fact, it's one of my beliefs that California wines have outsold French wines in recent years—not because California wines necessarily taste better, but because we can more easily pronounce the names of California wines and then order them with confidence. You can see the problem with *Clos du Bois*; this wine is produced by a California company that has adopted a difficult French name. It seems as if they spend twenty-five seconds out of every thirty-second commercial teaching Americans how to pronounce the name. Other examples abound, from *Frothe* to *Remifemin* to *Liebfraumilch*. Remember, customers never want to look stupid or inept.

Author Nick Haraway's first novel was initially entitled *The Wages of Gonzo Lubitsch*, but it was just too hard to pronounce. Even in personal settings, he kept having to repeat the title. Inevitably, the book was published as *The Gone-Away World*. Remember the movie *Gigli?* Obviously, few people saw the movie and virtually none of them could pronounce it. And, here's one of my favorite examples that easily turns into a tongue twister: *Sea World's Ship Wreck Rapids*. Say that name five times and tell me how you do. It's a classic illustration of how not to name.

5. Easy to Remember: Alliterations are good devices to increase memory recall. Jeff Jordan of *Mindset Research* has a name that just goes together, as does speaker Zig Ziegler, make-up artist Bobbie Brown or singer Joan Jett. Rhymes also work as in *Jelly Belly, Flower Power, Slim Jim*, etc.

6.Clearly Identifiable: Many names sound alike. In the pharmaceutical sphere, compare Celebrex with Celebex, Taxol to Paxol, or Nicoderm to Nitroderm. Take a highly stressful hospital environment along with most doctors' unreadable handwriting and you have a prescription for disaster. It's no wonder that so many wrongful death suits, as a result of mixed up medications, have been successfully won by patients.

In the cyber world, there are over 25,000 companies that have the word "micro," "cyber," or "net" in their names. Even in my industry, I'm plagued by competitors like Interbrand, The Brand Consultancy, Brand Institute, Brand Fidelity, Brand Equity, or ABC Name Bank, Name Lab, Name It, Nameslingers and Name Base. They all sound the same!

7. Free from Associations: Some words have such a strong association with another name that they must be avoided. Take Absolut, for example. Absolut equals vodka. When I hear of all of the new products with the word "absolute," I still think of vodka!

How about the company Edison Security? The word "Edison" is so associated with the electric company that the security company has to post this disclaimer at the end of every single piece of communication: "Edison Security is not the same company as Southern California Edison, the utility, and is not regulated by the California Public Utilities Commission. You do not have to buy Edison Security products in order to continue to receive quality regulated services from the utility."

Or, consider Woolworths, a chain of furniture stores in Britain, which introduced "Lolita," a bed targeted for 6-year-old girls. Yikes! The retailer claimed to have never heard of the famous 1955 novel in which the narrator becomes way too involved with his 12-year-old stepdaughter. Really?

And of course, look at Burlington Coat Factory. Read the disclaimer at the end of every commercial—"not affiliated with Burlington Industries."

Avoid a Name If a Huge Brand Also Uses the Name

Consider the words "Jiff" or "Jiffy." No matter how you conjugate them (and I have tried) they conjure up Jif peanut butter, Jiffy Lube, or Jiffy Popcorn. Trinity Hill recently removed the signature of its winemaker, John Hancock, from its bottles after the behemoth John Hancock Life Insurance Co. thought consumers might be confused. How about the term "Powership"? Federal Express is the 900-pound gorilla in that space making it difficult to create a variation on the term.

When Bad Names Happen to Good Products

Sometimes bad names are created and it's too late to change them—they have too much of what the industry calls "brand equity." In that case, your only hope is to try to turn lemons into lemonade. Pam, the non-stick cooking spray, unveiled commercials in early 2002 that played off its unusual name. Banter included the question, "Who made the breakfast?" Answer: "Pam did!"

Or, suppose your name is just three letters. ING hit a home run with its clever ads implying that half of its name was hidden behind bus benches or obscured by a building. Its tagline became "Not just an ending; a beginning."

One of the most inappropriately named products has got to be Britney Spears perfume. After a year of meltdown when she lost custody of her children for a while, shaved her head, and was forcibly sent to the hospital, her perfume appeared on store shelves with this misnomer: "In Control." Ha! Do you think it's a good fit?

A new online dating service was recently introduced via talk shows. After listening for over ten minutes, I still couldn't understand the exact brand name. It was Cybersuitors. Say it aloud and you'll hear what I mean.

WORDS of "LIZDOM"

NOM SEQUITURS

Make sure to avoid nom sequiturs; taken from the Latin expression of non sequiturs, this is my new expression meaning a brand name that doesn't follow, one that doesn't fit the personality of the brand.

Other products have been launched that are the exact opposite of what their name says. Looking for your caffeine fix? Don't try Cafix; it's a 100 percent caffeine-free beverage. Or, take a look at Aspercreme; this medication doesn't contain any aspirin. Smirnoff Ice is under scrutiny because most consumers, obviously, assume that it contains vodka. Right? Wrong! The back of the bottle states that it is a "flavored beer." Clorox Wipes seem like the ideal method to clean and disinfect. The only problem is that the wipes don't contain bleach!

How about this inappropriate name? Hendrix Vodka. Didn't Hendrix die with vodka in his system? Isn't this like Mama Cass endorsing a line of ham sandwiches?

These are all examples of nom sequiturs. Nom Sequiturs occur when you have a name that is not suitable, or inappropriate for the market. Digex sounds just like an aid for indigestion, but it is a Web hosting service. Dynasty Suites sounds like a perfect, upscale place to stay until you find that it is just off of a busy highway and that the rooms are just $39 per night.

ADW—Acronyms Don't Work

Although acronyms are technically initials that spell words (ex: MADD), they have morphed today into any string of initials. The biggest issue with them is that they are 30 percent less memorable than real words. There is also the matter of sound confusion as well. On the phone, for instance, it's hard to tell if the caller is saying "IP" or "IB" and "emcee" or "MC." This exact problem happened to me while I was doing a consulting project for HNC Software (now owned by Fair Isaac). My marketing research respondents thought I was saying "agency" instead of the correct company name. Hear the problem?

You should strive to avoid acronyms for your company name, even if you think it is simply for internal purposes only. Many of us have learned the hard way that an internal name often quickly makes its way to the outside world. At least that's what happened in 1994 when Apple decided to call its new operating system "Dylan." Bob Dylan sued, claiming trademark infringement. Apple counter-argued that it was an internal name only and that it actually stood for "dynamic language." Suffice it to say that Apple and Dylan reached a confidential out-of-court settlement.

And, acronyms often end up being used pejoratively. IBM was often referred to during its massive layoff as "I've Been Moved." SAP, the big German enterprise software maker, was known as "Stand up And Pay." And, even words that weren't acronyms became them when the products underperformed: SPAM: Stuff Parading as Meat, FORD: Fix Or Repair Daily or the EDSEL: Every Day Something Else Leaks.

Many executives will argue that acronyms certainly haven't hurt the success of IBM, GE, or AT&T. However, these companies have a history of invention that, in many ways, truly changed the business world. One estimate is that all of AT&T's advertising expenditures to date are over $65 billion! Further, these letters really do stand for real words: International Business Machines, General Electric, and American Telephone and Telegraph, respectively.

Do I think many companies have successfully created acronyms? You betcha! Would I recommend it today as a solution for your small business? No. It takes vast amounts of resources to imbue letters with brand meaning, emotion, and promise.

The two successful companies that have turned bad names into stars are AFLAC and GEICO. American Family Life Assurance Co. catapulted its domestic name recognition of approximately 2 percent in 1990 to approximately 80 percent now, thanks to the famous AFLAC duck. The duck is so famous that even Ben Affleck, during an appearance on David Letterman's show, starting making fun of his own name! Government Employees Insurance Company (GEICO) introduced the now-famous gecko in 1999 during the Screen Actors Guild strike that prevented the use of live actors. Voila! The talking mascot was born.

MYELITA MELTON

Myelita Melton started her company as a sole proprietorship in October 1998 under the brand name SpeakEasy Communications, which focused on teaching Spanish to English speakers in the workplace. The first Web site was SpanishforGringos.com with a "Mexican Sleeping Man" as her logo. Myelita never felt comfortable with the image or the Web site name, but customers loved it! Seven years later, with the goal of expanding distribution of her Spanish book series to Amazon, libraries, and colleges, this entrepreneur changed the site to SpeakEasySpanish.com and dropped her trademarked logo for a new one featuring a prickly pear cactus. Did it work? Let's be clear: since the brand change, her revenues have heated up 30 percent.

Remember, if you create a great name, then you're on the right road to creating a legacy.

When to Change Your Name

Changing a brand name is serious business; you must weigh the positives of a new name against the negatives of losing any derived brand equity. Yet it happens all the time. Recent estimates show that approximately 25,000 companies change their name every year. Foodmaker took on the brand name of its fast-food outlets: Jack in the Box; Consolidated Foods took the best known name out of its pantry and became Sara Lee; Arthur Andersen was forced to change its name when it spun off its consulting business and became Accenture; and it's hard to imagine that our favorite "document company," Xerox, was once the Haloid Corporation.

WORDS of "LIZDOM"

CHANGING A BRAND NAME

In changing a brand name, you must weigh the positives of a new name against the negatives of losing any derived brand equity.

SUDS

And, do you think Paradise Island would have been so successful a destination if it had kept its original name of Hog Island? Or would we have the over-fishing problem if the Patagonian tooth fish had not transformed into Chilean sea bass? And does escargot sound more appetizing than snails?

Alice Cooper, nee Vince Furnier, boasts that changing his name was one of his most brilliant career moves. He admits that "The concept of a male playing the role of an androgynous witch in tattered clothes and wearing make-up would cause social controversy and grab headlines."

Jerry Swain learned the hard way how a name with unintended connotations can restrict distribution and sales. He created his melt-in-your mouth peanut butter and chocolate product in college and called it *Jer's IncrediBalls*, but big box retailers wouldn't accept the product. The brand name was in conflict with the high image and high price he was seeking. After changing the name to *Jer's Gourmet Handmade Chocolate*, he easily earned distribution at Neiman Marcus, Vons, and even as an in-and-out item at Costco.

Change Your Name If a Negative Connotation Can Be Derived from Your Brand

Do you remember the '70s appetite suppressant, Ayds? Obviously, chewing the caramel candies doesn't transmit AIDS, but the tie-in between the brand and the disease obviously hit consumers hard. It died a quick death.

One successful example of a rebranding effort is the mono unsaturated oil originally named rapeseed. Clearly, that word has huge negative associations. The answer? Rename it canola oil!

Some brands are just sitting ducks for creating negative associations. Take the Drury hotel chain, for example. It's just too easy to translate the name into Dreary. Can you imagine how much more successful the chain could be if it had a different name? Or, consider the company named Rodopi. Although named after a mountain range, saying it fast sounds as if you're saying, "we're dopey." Yes, and where's Grumpy? And thank goodness Ponzi Marketing finally changed its name to Open Mind Marketing.

My company helped to change the name of the Denver Postal Credit Union, a 70-year-old credit union originally formed just for postal workers. There were a myriad of reasons for the change: they had branches outside of Denver, consumers thought they were affiliated with the US government, members tried to mail letters at its branches, non-members assumed they couldn't join if they weren't postal workers, and of course, the negative connotation of the term "go postal." We changed its name to Eagle Legacy. The new name extends the legacy of the credit union's ties with the US Postal Service by borrowing the familiar eagle, while at the same time reflecting the Spirit of the West. Its new tagline, "Your Wings of Financial Security," completes the credit union's new brand image.

The Nuancing Group also changed the name of the Child Abuse Prevention Foundation to Promises 2 Kids. Why? Because the original name was long and confusing, the organization was kicked off MySpace for "promoting child abuse" (absurd!), and checks kept pouring in made out to the wrong organization! Today, the name is easier and truly delivers upon the organization's promise to protect our children.

Now, here's a company that had a political firestorm brewing and made a change for the better. Beaner's Coffee, established in 1975, changed its name to Biggby Coffee to avoid any connection to an Hispanic slur. This change smells like the right move to me!

A budding entrepreneur in college decided to drop the common-place name Stephanie and instead tried using her initials with an exclamation point. Boom! SAM! was born. Today, SAM! is group president of Kforce Professional Staffing Information Management division.

FAITH POPCORN

RED HOT EXAMPLE

Faith Popcorn always had a vision of what she wanted to do—become a trend forecaster. She even coined the term "cocooning" to refer to the phenomenon of curling up in our houses. But her first step was to make a name for herself, and she did. She abandoned the surname name of Plotkin, and then her career really popped!

Change Your Name If It Is Connected to Insurmountable Negative Publicity

Often it seems that it's easier to rename a company than to change its perception. It's also easier to convince the customer that you have a product innovation under a new brand than trying to flag it as "new!" or "improved!" The brand name Valeant was recently unveiled to replace ICN Pharmaceuticals, a company that was tainted by the stock misappropriations of its founder.

When ValuJet crashed into the Everglades in the tragic May 1996 accident that killed all 110 passengers, its reputation was decimated. It became even worse after the Federal Aviation Administration started scrutinizing its safety records. After ValuJet purchased AirTrans Airways in 1997, the decision was easy—adopt the smaller airline's name and forever banish the brand name and its smiling face logo. In fiscal 2009, AirTrans is the number-two discount airline, and has earned a $10 million profit while its direct competitor lost $1.3 billion.

Avoiding Genericide

If you were christened with a name like John Smith, or Jane Baker, good for you. These names are rarely misspelled (duh!) and are easy to say. Now for the bad news: they render you invisible in Google. You are surrounded by hundreds of thousands of others with the same brand name, and it becomes impossible to find you! Welcome to the digital age: if you can't be easily "googled" and found, you don't exist!

WORDS of "LIZDOM"

NAMING FOR A DIGITAL WORLD

In today's world you don't exist unless you can be found quickly and easily on the Web. Before deciding on a name, check out the search results.

SUDS

So, for example, if I want to impress one of my clients, Kathy Clark, and find her skeletons in the closet, I'm in for a gambling game because there are over 500,000 hits. Where do I start? See the problem?

One way to solve this problem is to create a descriptive-type brand name such as these folks:

HELLO
my name is

"The Organizer Lady"
a.k.a., Sandra Felton

BIRTH NAME	SUCCESSFUL DESCRIPTIVE NAME
Sandra Felton	"The Organizer Lady"
Phil Lempert	"Supermarket Guru"
Bill Marvin	"The Restaurant Doctor"
Bud Bilanich	"The Common Sense Guy"
Wesley Ford	"That Value Guy"
Cedric Kyles	"Cedric the Entertainer"
Daniel Lawrence Whitney	"The Cable Guy"
Deena Stacer	"The Real Estate Doctor"

SUSAN FRIEDMANN

Susan Friedmann began her consulting and speaking business in 1989 under the brand name Diadem Communications and faced two distinct problems: 1) Most folks didn't know what a diadem was (I didn't, but it is the name of the famous Greek laurel wreath worn around the head). 2) It didn't tell prospects what services she provided. So, after ten years, she switched her brand to The Tradeshow Coach. Today, by virtue of her descriptive name, she earns high Google rankings when Web visitors are looking for tradeshow assistance. Susan has written more than ten books, including Secrets of Successful Exhibiting and Riches in Niches. Her newsletter focuses on that niche, and you'll find her today speaking at tradeshows as well as espousing the power of them. Sizzling niche!

Become a One-Name Show

I often think that Beyoncé went through elementary school absolutely hating her name, since teachers and schoolmates called her "beyonds." But now, her unique moniker has allowed her to go simply by one name.

WORDS of "*LIZ*DOM"

GO FOR ONE NAME

If your name is unique enough, but still relatively easy to say and easy to spell, then explore if you can drop your last name. It worked for Cher, Beyoncé, Madonna, and Seal.

Can you go by one name? You can, if your name straddles the line between special, yet simple to say. And think about a unique spelling as well. Shortening Cheryl to Cher became a signature for this outrageous entertainer. And I don't know about you, but I have never met another Madonna before. The strategy also works well for Bono (born as Paul Hewson), Prince (born Prince Nelson—really!), and Sting (born Gordon Matthew Sumner). With a given name like Seal Henry Olusegun Olumide Adelo Samuel, it's easy to see why Seal works best.

KRISHNA

Krishna Walker always faced the raised eyebrow about her name. "Is your name really Krishna?" Yes. "Like the Hindu deity?" Yes. As an expert in body work, she discovered that in her fifth year of business, it no longer became relevant to give her last name. In fact, just hearing her first name was enough. Now, she a successful one-name brand!

Turn a Lemon Name into Lemonade Success

Perhaps you were born with an uncommon name, but don't want to change it for a host of reasons. You can use its distinctiveness to your advantage. Most of us in California, for example, have mastered how to say Arnold Schwarzenegger and can even mimic his accent! Robin Bottomley, Vicki Turnipseed, and Paul Hoeprich have each used their name to its best advantage. I even like the way Rick Butts uses his name—"kicking the butts out of life" at all of his speaking engagements.

The Power of Nicknames

Nicknames are tremendously powerful. You only come up with them if you care about a brand. If you're indifferent, you won't waste a moment creating one. Most importantly, however, nicknames are a sign of endearment: You are so special that you deserve a special name. Bloomingdale's has become Bloomies (at least in my house!), Nordstrom transformed into Nordies, McDonald's morphed into Mickey D's, BMW was shortened to Beemer, Federal Express became FedEx, Beverages & More was shortened to BevMo, and Target magically became French with the pronunciation of Tar-zhay. Jennifer Lopez is now simply J Lo. As you'll note, most of these nicknames are shorthand. Why? Because we like short, easy names.

If you're still struggling with a catchy name, think back into your childhood. Ask your parents, siblings, and childhood mates the names they recall about you. One of the most unusual nicknames I've found is *Brip Blap*. It's from the movie *How to Murder Your Wife*. The character has huge emotional mood swings, bripping and blapping all over the place. Apparently, *Steve* (semi-anonymous as the blogger of BripBlap.com) had the same swings as a child and the moniker stuck!

In her childhood, Nancy Coker was wild about noodles (before we called it pasta). Her father coined her nickname "The Noodler" and even gave her a new car with that phrase on the vanity license plate. The name stuck, and now Noodler Entertainment plays off the noodle in your brain as she creates fun, intelligent birthday party treasure hunts.

Sometimes names are bestowed upon you based on your special talent or skill, especially in sports. Adam Jones moves so fast around the football field that he earned the nickname Pac Man Jones. William Perry earned his nickname—*The Refrigerator*—by virtue of his gargantuan frame. In the 2008 Olympic Games, after breaking world records for both the 100- and 200-meter dash, Usain Bolt was quickly christened The Lightning Bolt. Even the entire US basketball team was dubbed "The Redeem Team" as it blew away its competitors and reclaimed the gold medal.

The moniker "Superwoman" was bestowed upon asset manager Nicola Horlick who runs a London-based asset fund, raised her children, and then fought off armed robbers outside her home. Wow!

Look at some of these famous singers:

HELLO
my name is

"First Lady of Soul"
a.k.a., Aretha Franklin

BIRTH NAME	PERFORMANCE NAME
Aretha Franklin	First Lady of Soul
Michael Jackson	King of Pop
James Browne	King of Soul
Bruce Springsteen	The Boss
Kitty Wells	The Queen of Country Music
Frank Sinatra	Chairman of the Board
Glenn Campbell	Rhinestone Cowboy

Welcome to Naming Architecture

Relax, naming architecture is simple. It just requires a little forethought in launching your first product or service to ensure that successive products relate.

The easy example to illustrate this point is McDonald's. You can order Chicken McNuggets, McSkillet Burrito, an Egg McMuffin, and of course, the Big Mac! The prefix "Mc" is the unifying theme of the brand. Frito Lay works the suffix end of the equation and creates chips that end in "itos," such as Fritos, Doritos, Cheetos, and Tostitos. Boyd Gaming used to own the Gold Coast, the Suncoast, and the Barbary Coast. Steve Jobs went down this path initially by calling the company "Apple," its first product "McIntosh," and its PDA "Newton." But, it abandoned this strategy altogether with the birth of the I-Pod.

Why is naming architecture important? Because customers often don't remember the company's name or the author's name or the manufacturer's name; they just remember the product. By creating a family of related brands, you let everyone know that you are the parent!

I know, for example, that every Lillian Braun book title will start with "*The Cat Who...*" Each fabulous Sophia Kinsella book in the series will be entitled "*Shopaholic and...*" Every Jack Canfield book will be entitled "*Chicken Soup for the...*" (At this point, I think there is a *Chicken Soup for the Chicken's Soul* in the works!)

Then, of course, there is J.K. Rowling, who literally changed the face of Scholastic Books and young adult book publishing with her breakthrough series about Harry Potter. Each and every book was met with even more frenzied demand, "leaks" on the Web, midnight release dates, and an aura of magic. Thank you Rowling for putting young adult literature back onto the main stage and creating the naming architecture of "*Harry Potter and the...*" series.

An unusual twist on naming architecture is to bend your own brand name. Dannon created its kid-oriented line of drinkable yogurts under the brand name Danimals. Reebok had a children's line it called Weeboks (love that name!). Nestle often uses its prefix as in NESCAFE. And, M&M's, a perennial chocolate favorite, offers customers the chance to become an M-bassador when they participate in frequent surveys to provide feedback. Don't forget about my cult favorite: Peet's Coffee. When you become a passionate fan, you become a Peetnik—a great twist on its brand along with its San Francisco, bohemian heritage.

The Five Deadly Sins of Naming:

Deadly Sin #1: Holding a Naming Contest

Inevitably, when it's time to create a new brand or company name, someone comes up with the brilliant idea to hold a naming contest. Actually, it's not so brilliant. If the contest is either among employees or even at a trade booth, the time actually spent on the project is disproportionate to its value. Isn't a new name worth more than five minutes of thought while uncomfortably standing on a trade show floor?

Even worse, contestants usually don't understand naming rules or linguistics. They rarely know your naming preferences, the competitive landscape, trademark law, domain availability, or constructional linguistics to ensure that your name is appropriate and available. You then feel compelled to use the name and award a prize, even though you know that there is no winner in this game.

This scenario is exactly what happened to The Bankers Bank in 2007 when it was considering a name change. It blasted out this criteria to employees: the domain had to be available, the name had to be available for trademark, and the brand could not have the words "bankers bank" in its new name. What a surprise! A whopping 123 employees submitted entries, and not one single name submitted was used. Instead, the bank (since renamed Silverton Bank) put all of the contestants' names in a hat, and luck determined which one received the $500 consolation prize. Oh, and the bank still had to hire a branding firm to create a new name.

Deadly Sin #2: Creating a Name for the Moment

Your goal in naming is to create a brand that will survive the long term: a name that will survive today and prosper tomorrow.

Consider *20th Century Insurance*, *Boston Chicken*, and even *Modem Media*. All of these names were developed with a very narrowing, limiting focus. Didn't the insurance company believe they'd be around in the new millennium? Or, if the business plan for Boston Chicken called for expanding into turkey and ham, shouldn't the company have named the restaurant correctly the first time? Is Modem Media ready to change its name to Broadband Media?

Deadly Sin #3: Forgetting the International Audience

The Internet has truly made naming a worldwide event. All names today must work in numerous languages, or at least in the most common ones. One California-based Internet company continues to lead the pack of Web sites designed to help you create invitations, plan the event, and accept reservations. It christened itself Evite. The issue? Evite, stemming from the Spanish verb "evitar," means to avoid, abandon, or shun. And fully 35 percent of the population in California is Hispanic! Then there's the classic story, circulated around the globe, of how Chevrolet introduced the car, Nova, into Spanish speaking countries where nova translates into "no go." Recently, however, statistics have emerged showing astonishingly strong sales in Latin America, lending credence to the theory that the story might just be an urban legend.

Nissan didn't learn from Chevy's misstep. It designed a spectacular electric concept car that's winning raves. And its name is...*Pivo*. But wait a minute! "*Pivo*" means beer in most Slavic languages. What a concept indeed! Have a beer and keep on truckin'! Toyota also missed the boat with MR2. In French, it translates as if reading the words "mer" plus "deux"—meaning "sh*t." Oops!

I also chuckle when I remember how Israel mistakenly translated the sentence "Jerusalem: there's no place like it" from Hebrew to English. The tagline then morphed into "Jerusalem: There is no such city."

Some foreign language mistakes continue to be made over and over again. Esteé Lauder introduced Country Mist, Rolls Royce introduced the Silver Mist, and Clairol introduced the Mist Stick. The only problem was that the word "mist" in German roughly translates into horse manure! How alluring!

Deadly Sin #4: Not Investing in Trademark Review

Legal forethought now can save you from legal headaches later. When you're developing a name against a tight budget and a deadline, it's easy to dismiss the legal ramifications of a name. After all, you believe that since you thought of the name, no one else has. But, be forewarned: legal problems can cost your business thousands of dollars! Trademark law is based upon the concept of "confusingly similar." If a customer is likely to confuse two brands with each other or believe that they are made by the same company, the Court will usually invoke this legal standard and rule that there is trademark infringement. To determine who has the right to the name, the law finds in favor of the brand that has the earliest documentation of its first use. Remember, even if a name is not registered with the US Patent and Trademark Office, it still retains some form of trademark protection. Of course, most intellectual property lawyers will tell you that you should register all of your trademarks.

Deadly Sin #5: Squishing Two Brand Names Together

Afraid of losing brand name recognition in the wake of a merger? Just combine all of the names together. You'll join the tongue-twisting ranks of Dean Witter Morgan Stanley, ExxonMobil, LVMH Moet Hennessy Louis Vuitton, DaimlerChrysler, PricewaterhouseCoopers, Bristol-Myer Squibb, AOL Time Warner and SmithKline Beecham. Name merging is the compromise solution chosen when neither party will agree to a new company moniker. Although it retains the brand equity of both companies, a new identity is never created, leading to the infighting that has pitted the young turks against the old school in the AOL/Time Warner merger.

YOUR TURN TO ACT

Google your exact name in quotes. Review the results to determine the quantity of the hits and the competitors occupying your space. Warning: my girlfriend discovered that although she had a very cool, interesting name— Krickett—it was also the name of a big porn star who steals the show on search engines.

Have a trip down memory lane with old friends and family. Ask them to recall any early nicknames for you. Muffy, Skip, Wild Jack, or RJ may just be the name answer you're looking for.

Investigate your name with a combination of any description of what you do. Ex: Bill the Plumber, The Cool, Pool Guy, the Queen of Rock, etc.

Review your proposed name in at least Spanish, French, German, Italian, and Chinese or Japanese. Start with the Web and then use your e-mail contacts to connect you with someone who can do a quick, easy, and free reality check.

Find a name to fit your business for the long term. Unless you don't think your company is going to survive this century, don't name it 21st Century Insurance, for example. Or, if you're going to expand your offerings, keep your name broad enough for future growth.

     Liz Goodgold

Chapter 4

Fire Starters:
Understanding the Basics of Intellectual Property

STRIKE the MATCH

Pair the correct individual with the famous brand that was sued for trademark or copyright infringement.

INDIVIDUAL/COMPANY	BRAND NAME
1. Art Buchwald sues for copyright infringement	A Coming to America (movie)
2. H&R Block sues for infringement on its "we got people" tagline	B Haute Diggity Dog
3. Cisco sues over trademark infringement on I-phone name it registered in 2000	C American Express
	D Uptowne Productions
4. Burberry sues over infringing upon its trademarked plaid	E Apple
5. Blue Man Group sues promoter over booking a production that has all of the actors in blue face.	F Iconix
6. Adidas files suit against shoe discounter for infringing upon its 3-stripe trademark logo.	G Payless Shoes
7. Luxury luggage giant Luis Vuitton sues dog toy called Chewy Vuitton	

It is often stated that a little information is dangerous, and in this case, where there's smoke, there's fire! A little trademark knowledge will help you sidestep some of the mines in the naming field. Of course, this is also the area where my own lawyer will make me write the disclaimer that you should seek the full counsel of a lawyer before relying upon this advice. (Yikes! Lawyers!)

Trademark Infringement vs. Mindshare Infringement

Intellectual Property (IP) lawyers are quick to tell you about the risks of treading in waters already occupied by a competitor. In fact, if you are at the beginning stages of naming your company, you are best served by not using any name that sounds even remotely familiar to another brand unless you truly have the resources to defend the mark. Most new businesses, small businesses, and home-based businesses make this recommendation a foregone conclusion. Even if you and the similarly named company operate in two distinctly different areas of business, you run the risk of being sued and issued a "cease and desist" letter.

MONEY SAVING TIP Before taking your proposed short list to an Intellectual Property lawyer for review, perform a free search yourself at the US Patent and Trademark Office (uspto.gov). Then, if it clears that hurdle, you might want to order directly an extensive trademark review that includes state marks directly from a research company.

If you call your company McWellness, as one health consulting firm did in Boston, expect to be shut down rather quickly by McDonald's. If you're like Elizabeth McCaughey and had a coffee shop for 17 years under the name McCoffee, also be prepared to lose to this consumer giant. It is zealous and some would argue overly litigious about its trademark.

As we learned in the previous chapter, McDonald's uses the "Mc" prefix to denote most of its products. Naming architecture is revered by trademark lawyers, because it easily refers and reinforces the source of the goods. That's why, for example, Toys R Us, Babies R Us, and Kids R Us have so successfully defended its trademark. The backwards R and unusual term "R us" make trademark infringement easy to prove.

TRADER JOE'S

Trader Joe's, a privately held grocery chain, has an almost cult-like following in the states where it has stores. Its positioning is to provide really healthy, great tasting food at unbelievable prices. Want to try wild bay scallops? All natural kettle corn? Crustless quiche? Hmmm, it's all here backed with this guarantee: "if you don't like it, bring it back." Its private labels all use a twist on naming architecture, calling its brand Trader Darwin (for vitamins), Trader Jose (for Mexican food), Trader Giotto (for Italian food), and Trader Ming for (for Chinese food). Bon appetite!

AT&T fizzled with a very unsuccessful campaign called "mLife." It soon got the attention of the Metropolitan Life Insurance Company, which quickly claimed infringement and the ad quickly went up in smoke.

Red Bull tried to pull a fast one. It filed an application to register "bull-shi*t" as a trademark. It argued unsuccessfully that it could also be construed as "Bull's Hit," but the Trademark Examiner found that argument entirely unpersuasive. The Board concluded: "the term is offensive to the conscience of a substantial composite of the general public."

WORDS of "*LIZ*DOM"

MINDSHARE INFRINGEMENT

Never tread into a competitor's space with a confusingly similar name. If your brand name triggers thoughts about your competitor, and you don't have the deep pockets necessary to defend the mark, you could be playing with fire! Choose a different moniker.

There are many nuances to the legal definition of trademark infringement, but I believe that there is also "mindshare infringement." My standard is that if your marketing messages trigger a thought about your competitor, abandon ship!

Sea World proudly introduced a few seasons ago an amazing act at its parks featuring outrageous outfits, mystifying Chinese acrobats, ethereal music, and bouts of humor called "Cirque de le Mer." Sound familiar? Even the spelling reminds me of the ubiquitous Cirque du Soleil. And how about the body lotion called Avoplex? Makes you think it is made by Avon, right?

Jeep started a commercial with this voice-over: "There is only one Amazon." Of course, I immediately thought of Amazon.com. Fujitsu began another ad with "Web hosting needed ASAP." Again, I thought of a different product: SAP.

I recently met a "life coach" whose business card boasted that she helps people move from "good to great." Hey! Isn't that way too similar to Jim Collins' bestseller *Good to Great*? I think so.

Neology Meets Its Match

NEOLOGY

Neology is the science of creating new words. Verizon, Nuprin, Vantage, and Maxima are all good examples.

Neology is a cool word that just means the science of creating new words. Hey, your kid might even be an expert, especially in their formative years. Inventing new words is a solid path to a brand name because of two key reasons: 1) it has strong trademark protection and 2) if you invented a new word, it's easy to get the domain.

Verizon counts as a neologism, as does Vaio, Muccinex, Wellbutrin, VapoRub, Nuprin, Alli, and virtually every single drug in your medicine cabinet. You can also invent new words by dropping a prefix or letter as in the cases of Abreva, Maxima, Acura, and Advanta. I like putting a new twist on an old name as in the case of Mike's Hard Lemonade, which introduced its version of a margarita and called it Mike-arita. Try combining two words together and you get brands such as Metabolife, Epicurious, Tejava, and Vividence. We created the brand names Aquinity for a water-delivery drug mechanism and Eclicktic for software used by furniture industry.

MILO SHAPIRO

RED HOT
EXAMPLE

Milo Shapiro is an expert in improvisation and in using improv techniques in business applications, such as team building. He started his company in 2000 with the brand name: "ImproVentures," a great merger of "improvise" and "ventures." The only problem remaining, however, was the mispronunciation. Readers were seeing it as ImproveVentures. When he changed the capitalization to IMPROVentures, presto! He achieved the right combination of the brand name and the right pronunciation!

Names of Whimsy

Fanciful or whimsical names are another tried and true path to successful naming. It is as if you take a word and apply it to a brand that has no relationship whatsoever to the product or service. Blue Rhino makes and exchanges propane tanks, usually used for backyard BBQ grills. And, unless you routinely see this imaginary animal, it counts as a fanciful name per trademark law. Red Bull also uses the colored animal approach for its high-octane drink. Chippendales, as literally branded on the gorgeous hunks of the male dance show, have no relation to the style of furniture from which their name is borrowed. Oracle is defined as a prophetic opinion or even a revelation from God, but most of us now think of the software enterprise company. Quick silver is mercury, but with a quick elimination of the "c" it becomes Quiksilver, the hip manufacturer of surf clothes.

How Names Sound

Your hope is that your brand name will be more often spoken aloud than read. If so, it means that you are building buzz, people are talking about you, or they are even on YouTube discussing your brand. This discussion therefore merits a brief overview of "sound alikes."

It's more important how your brand sounds than how it is printed, at least according to the US Patent & Trademark Office, the US government agency that regulates trademarks. How people hear your brand is critical. Using the Web only, therefore to test a name is destined for failure. Why? Because unless you use software that includes sound for pronunciation , you are only gauging how words are spelled and not how the reader is thinking they will sound.

When I was working on a new brand name for HNC Software (now a part of Fair Isaac, the folks who control your FICO score), we tested the brand name Shop Wave. If we had merely tested it online, we never would have uncovered the fact that most respondents spelled back "Shock Wave," the Macromedia trademark. And when testing Tall Stone as another company's name, it rather unfortunately came back as "gall stone." It was immediately "cut" from the list!

WORDS of "*LIZ*DOM"

SUDS

TESTING YOUR NAME ALOUD

Before finalizing a brand name, make sure to test how it sounds. Ask a number of people to spell back exactly what you said. If they consistently say another brand or hear the name incorrectly, try again.

YOUR TURN TO ACT

Testing Recall—Call your Council individually and read them your short list of proposed brand names. Ring them back exactly one week later and remind them of your phone call about brands. Without giving up any information, ask them if they can remember any of the names proposed. The one that is most frequently recalled, unaided, is probably the winner.

Testing Confusingly Similar—In the same phone call, after you say each name aloud, ask the listener to spell back to you exactly what he or she heard. Look for misspellings (important in Chapter 6 where we talk about domain registration) or any confusion with another brand.

Check with an Intellectual Property lawyer about registering a trademark on your brand.

Chapter 5

Master of Your Domain
Heating Up Your Brand in Cyberspace

Not all companies have their name as their .com;
pair the brand with its domain:

BRAND	DOMAIN
1. Kellogg's Rice Krispies	A verbivore.com
2. Law firm of Morrison & Foerster	B themythinglink.com
3. Phoenix Consulting	C ilovebeer.com
4. World Wresting Entertainment	D snapcracklepop.com
5. Richard Lederer	E therock.com
6. Oscar Mayer	F bologna.com
7. Corona Beer	G mofo.com

Yes, All the Good Ones Have Been Taken

If you are finding it nearly impossible to pair your brand name idea to a .com domain, it's no surprise. There are approximately 80 million registered domains that end with .com. Here are a few more startling facts:

- Every possible two-character and three-character combination—including both letters and numbers—are taken.

- The 1,000 most common English words are registered.

- The 1,219 most common male names and the 2,841 most common female names as well as the 10,000 most common surnames have also been snatched up.

- The word "sex" appears in only 257,000 domains (or at least as of this writing!).

- The average length of a domain name is thirteen letters.

- The longest domain name allowed is sixty-three characters.

Dot Com Remains the Gold Standard

Regardless of the proliferation of top-level domains including .me, .biz, .net, .org, .coop and the like, dot com remains the domain of choice. Registering a .net or other domain signifies to your audience that you are a second choice candidate. In essence, you broadcast to the world that your first choice domain was taken and therefore you "settled" for another option. It's hard to win customers when their first impression is not a strong one.

WORDS of "*LIZ*DOM"

THE DOT COM RULES

The .com remains the gold standard when it comes to domains. Do not settle for other alternatives before you have explored every other option. Choosing a second-level domain is broadcasting to the world that you have settled for second best.

SUDS

Forever Changing Landscape

Top-level domains are being added every year. Besides .net and .org there is now .mobi (for mobile devices), .name (open to anyone), .jobs (for companies seeking to advertise a posting), and .travel (must be verified as a travel-related entity). There are proposals currently circulating for city domains as well. Although you may not have been able to obtain anniesflowers.com, you may be able to obtain anniesflowers.nyc. For small business owners and local businesses, this may be the best present domain option if the .com is unavailable. Analysts are predicting that in addition to city names for domains, you might also see category suffixes such as .books, .restaurant, .store, etc.

Another option is to explore purchasing your domain. Although in earlier years, domain names sold for millions (remember when sex.com sold for $12 million, or when diamond.com changed hands for $7.5 million?), if you do not have a generic name, you may be able to purchase it at a reasonable price. Since I work with both behemoth players and small businesses, I know that many domains are exchanged for as little as $2,000. Make an offer!

MONEY SAVING TIP *If you are a large company or work for a large company, do not try to negotiate a domain purchase via the headquarters' e-mail. The minute your e-mail from liz@ibm.com crosses the domain seller's desk, the price will skyrocket. Instead, all communication should originate from your small account at Hotmail, Gmail, or Yahoo!*

Also, try to avoid hyphens or unusual suffixes like "inc" or "co" at the end of your domain. Lawyers are particularly guilty of using the dreaded "llc" (limited liability corporation) in their domains. Ugh!

Someone who understands the value of consistent branding in cyberspace is Linda Bustos, e-commerce consultant and blogger for Get Elastic. Linda has been involved in e-commerce for over ten years and has learned what it takes to be well branded online. One of her key insights is that if you pick an avatar (a cyber representation of you), make sure it is appropriate for the long run. In other words, this is your online brand and should be chosen with just as much care as your name.

ARIANNA HUFFINGTON

Arianna Huffington is the woman behind the success of The Huffington Post. Started in 2005 when she was considered late to the Internet party, it has become an important Web player, not only for political news and blogs, but also as a good source for late-breaking events, contrarian views, and now, even information on going green, style, and entertainment. It was reborn as an "Internet newspaper" in early 2008 and, at last count, approximately 8 million people visit her site, making her a very hot brand in cyberspace.

Capture All Variations

Make sure to register all variations of your brand. You want likely misspellings, likely typos, and inverted names. For whatever reason, for example, I'm referred to at least once per week as Liz Goldgood rather than Liz Goodgold. Most importantly, capture the singular and the plural. Witness the case of Virtual Vineyard. It started a brand with that domain, but oops! It forgot the virtual vineyards (with an "s") and eventually had to purchase it for $1 million.

One overlooked reason for registering many variations of your brand name is cybersquatting. Whereas the term initially meant simply registering another brand's domain (ex: Coke.com) and then trying to sell it back to Coca-Cola, it now refers to sitting on confusingly similar domains and collecting pay-per-click dollars for advertisers. The big companies quickly fight back and typically win. A case in point: Dell. A third party registered dellfinancialservices.com and collected thousands of dollars before the computer giant shut them down. Or, look at "windowslivecare.com" and see if it doesn't masquerade as an official Microsoft site. The bottom line: ensure that all domain roads lead back to you.

Also, look for shorthand. The history of the Internet shows us that typists are lazy; shorter is better. Barnes & Noble eventually morphed into bn.com (and had the privilege of buying that domain), Déjà Vu became deja.com, and Monster Board became monster.com. Looking at abbreviations from the get-go is a good safeguard.

Even though I trust that you are not using your own personal name as the name of your business, register your first and last name anyway, if you can. Why? Domain names that are the exact match to the search query end up as number-one in the rankings, making you easy to find. Another key reason? They prevent anyone else from registering your name and turning it into a negative site about you. (Please see Chapter 12 for info on "online reputation management.") Owning your domain also prevents someone from registering it and then trying to sell it back to you. Witness the case of Christian Siriano, winner of Project Runway season four. His design unveiled in 2008 had to be labeled Christian V. Siriano because a cyber squatter was holding his name (without the middle initial) ransom for $10,000.

Be Weary and Wary of Homonyms and Heteronyms

We discussed in Chapter 3 the importance of how your brand name sounds when spoken aloud. If someone hears your brand name, what will he or she type into the browser? Be especially careful when using homonyms. Homonyms are simply words that sound the same, but are spelled differently. For example, say your brand is Homes for Sale. Did you register all of these?

- Homesforsale.com   • Home4sale.com   • Homesfoursale.com

Heteronyms are important because if readers see your name in print, will they pronounce it correctly? Led Zeppelin grappled with this very issue. Originally spelled Lead Zeppelin, too many folks pronounced it "lead" as in rhymes with "seed."

I remember an e-mail blast in 2006 with this subject line: "Polish Thanksgiving Specials!" I immediately thought it was related to Poland or someone's idea of a tasteless joke. It's impossible to know, and that's just the point. For clarity, the company should have added a modifier so that it read "Silver Polish," and then most readers would have known that MAAS was promoting its brand of cleaners and polishes.

NAME & DEFINITION   EXAMPLE

Homonym
Words that sound the same, but have different meanings and are spelled differently

Too, to, 2
Blue, blew
Bear, bare

Heteronyms
Words that are spelled the same, but are pronounced differently

Bow BAU— to lower one's head or the front of a ship; BOH—used to shoot arrows
Close CLOZE—to shut; CLOS—near

Your Name Must Work as a Domain

Another key guideline is to ensure that your brand name works as a domain. In other words, how does it look when all squished up together with a .com at the end. I remember early on in the Web days when a friend came to me so excited that he had registered his domain. I could hardly stop laughing when I realized he registered "billlloyd.com" That's right: four l's together in one domain. I suggested Williamlloyd.com. Look at these disasters:

NAME	DOMAIN EXAMPLE
Pen Island	Penisland.net (no comment)
Virus Exchange	Virusexchange.net (no thanks)
Campbell Go Red	Campbellgored.com (bull?)
Who Represents	Whorepresents.com (really?)
Donut Touch	donuttouch.com (do not touch)
Therapist Finder	therapistfinder.com (oh no!)
Speed of Art	Speedofart.com (excuse me!)
Go Tahoe	gotahoe.com (no comment!)
Vie Winery	viewinery (winery with a view?)

Pe

Invest in Auto Renew

Once you register your valuable domains, do not lose them! Most registrars (Go Daddy, Network Solutions, Inc., etc.) allow you to manage your domains through auto-renew. Take advantage of any system that will ensure that your domains are never lost for an oversight of payment.

SHEL HOROWITZ

Shel Horowitz is the author of more than three books on marketing, including Principled Profit and has learned the value of building his brand online. through Internet discussion groups. He follows these key rules: no flagrant self-promotion, participate regularly, no heated catfights, and always provide value.

YOUR TURN TO ACT

Register your own name and your brand name.

Capture the singular and the plural.

Ask your Council how they would spell your brand. Then, quickly register any of these variations, even if they are misspellings.

Think of any shorthand way your brand might be abbreviated, especially with an acronym; register those domains too.

Always use "auto renew" for all of your domains to keep your digital domain safe.

Chapter 6

Color My World
How to Ignite Your Brand with Color

Pair the correct color with the brand that made it famous:

COLOR	BRAND
1. Pink	A Tiffany
2. White	B Johnny Cash
3. Robin's Egg Blue	C Lance Armstrong
4. Brown	D Mary Kay
5. Blue	E IBM
6. Black	F UPS
7. Yellow	G Thomas Wolfe

Branding by Color

Our world revolves around color. Next time your friends get ready to prepare their cup of coffee, watch how they look for their sweetener: "blue" (Equal), "pink" (Sweet N' Low), or yellow (Splenda). They might even go so far as to ask a waiter if there is any of the "blue stuff."

This phenomenon of branding by color takes place even in the field of medicine. Patients will often tell their doctors that they take a blue little pill or a big yellow pill. Pharmaceutical manufacturers have the opportunity to use color as a way to help both consumers and doctors and as a way to reinforce their image. Besides the "purple pill" (Nexium), Nuprin was the first drug to try to "own" a rust-colored pill. Now, that color represents the entire category of ibuprofen, as evidenced by all similarly hued generic competitors. And Levoxyl, a thyroid medicine, according to Dr. Wendy Schilling, uses a stroke of branding genius by color coding its pills according to dosage.

Apparently, other women besides me are looking for that robin's egg blue-colored box during the holidays, signifying a gift from T & Co.—Tiffany. Just seeing the color triggers a 20 percent increase in the heart rate of American women. How's that for emotionally connecting with the brand?

And, the color of the cars we drive matters. A whopping 39 percent of car buyers will walk out of a showroom if their desired car color is not in stock! Currently, every GM car comes in twenty-two colors and almost 75 percent of its cars are available in orange. Clearly, orange is on trend this year.

New Zealand uses the color black fairly consistently to identify its sports teams: All Blacks is the name of the men's rugby team, the women's rugby team is the Black Ferns, the men's basketball team is The Tall Blacks, and the women's hockey team is the Black Sticks.

The singer Pink certainly created her brand name based upon her signature hair color. But, it was her hard-hitting style, no-holds-barred lyrics, and outspoken interviews that enabled her to build her brand image beyond her hairstyle. Today she boasts a platinum blonde look.

Since color acts as part of our personality, it's no surprise that as we develop, change, or even age, our color preferences change as well. For example, in 1993 Susan Macaulay moved from her home country of Canada to accompany her husband to Dubai. For ten years, she looked for work and lived a very comfortable existence. Then, ten years later, at the spur of the moment, she accepted a challenge by the not-for-profit *Gulf for Good* to tackle a 6-day, 120-kilometer trek on the wild side of the Great Wall of China. To get in shape for the trek, she had to create a healthier version of herself. After losing twenty pounds and conquering both the Great Wall of China and Mt. Kinabalu, she completely switched her wardrobe to body-hugging clothes and adopted the color pink as her signature color—a color she used to despise!

I remember meeting the founder of a "women in business" yellow pages directory-type company in Chicago. Her image is burnished in my mind: a spectacular yellow suit with a black silk blouse. She literally was her own walking mascot!

Author and speaker Jeffrey Gitomer has built an empire out of color coding his books: *Little Gold Book of Attitude, Little Red Book of Selling, Little Black Book of Connections*, etc.

SUSAN BURNASH

Susan Burnash has been in marketing for over twenty years, calling her first company Video Marketing One. When she moved to the State of Washington in January of 2008, she discovered that in trying to build a local client base, prospects didn't understand what business she was in and tended to forget the name of her company. Voila! In January of 2008, she switched her company name to Purple Duck Marketing, and her business hasn't stopped quacking since. She credits the enormous uptick in her business to her unusual name, which not only enables her to easily wear and use the color purple, but also functions as a great conversation starter. Way to stoke a fire, Susan!

The Psychology of Color

Color is a powerful tool; within three seconds of seeing something, we register its color and it thereby influences our perception. Dr. Marlene Siersema, talk show host, speaker, and author of *Marketing's Silent Language* explains that color is the silent language of communication that speaks louder and faster than the spoken word. In fact, color influences us in four key areas:

1. **Image** - It gives us an indelible impression.

2. **Health** – It affects both our physical and mental well-being

3. **Morale** - Color influences the emotional stability and performance in the work environment.

4. **Effectiveness** - Color has a strong impact on sales, production, longevity, customer loyalty, inventory control, product effectiveness, and employee effectiveness.

Before selecting a color for your brand, it's important to recognize that different colors trigger different feelings and emotions. English officials were pleased to note that the suicide rate tapered off significantly after changing the name of one of its bridges from black to blue. And here's a study that got my attention: invoices with a second color, and especially those with a blue border around the amount owed, are paid quicker than invoices issued in black and white.

Don't forget: the color you pick must also be consistent with the image you have in your mind and with your business plan.

The Psychology of Color

Color Symbolizes:

COLOR	SYMBOLIZES	EXAMPLE
Pink	Femininity, babies, soft	Mary Kay, Susan G. Komen, Barbie, Johnson & Johnson Baby Lotion
Red	Strength, vitality, rescue, danger	Target, Red Cross, Swiss Army
Orange	High energy, construction, movement	Home Depot, ING
Yellow	Light, future, philosophy	National Geographic, Yellow Tail
Green	Money, growth, environment, nature	Whole Foods, Starbucks, John Deere
Blue	Trust, authority, security	IBM, Microsoft, American Express
Purple	Royalty, spirituality, new age	Barney

Blue is, of course, the world's most popular color. Check out the next one hundred business cards you receive and see how high the percentage is within your circle. Blue Man Group has done a masterful job of cementing their image. They have even parlayed their success into a long-running gig in Vegas; a Swatch watch commercial; as spokesmen (who do not speak!) for Intel; and numerous other endorsements.

MONEY SAVING TIP *If you are down to a choice of one or two colors, investigate the in-stock availability of essential items. You might find, for example, that black envelopes are easy to find, while purple envelopes require special ordering and a special set-up fee.*

I remember having good chuckle when the Razr Chocolate phone was unveiled. Was it brown, the universal color of chocolate? No, it was black. Oy vey!

WORDS of "*LIZ*DOM"

COLOR

Pick a color or two for your brand that is appropriate for the brand personality and for the target market.

SUDS

Orange and red are high-energy colors. They are also considered appetite stimulants. No surprise then that most of the fast feeders such as Burger King, El Pollo Loco, and Sbarro use these colors to quickly turnover their sitting area.

AT&T is doing a good job of reinforcing its connection with the brand it gobbled up in 2007, Cingular, by adopting its singular color of orange. Veuve Clicquot's non-vintage champagne is called simply "orange label," and it even creates an orange purse as a premium during the holidays. Red soles are the sign of the very high-heeled and high priced Christian Louboutin shoes; you'll often see the flash of red on celebrity's feet; it's a great way to subtly brand.

Pink is an interesting color because women embrace it. In fact, it's become the signature color of women, as evidenced by the short-lived magazine entitled *Pink*, by the trademark color of Juicy Couture, and as the official color of the Susan B. Komen Foundation. For gobs of fun, take a look at the Sheila's Wheels Web site (www.sheilaswheels.com). It's completely targeted towards women (Sheila is slang for women in Australia), with handbag coverage and boasting "female friendly repairers." Note: pink is the most universally disliked color by men. Choose your colors according to your target to ensure you don't make any missteps.

When Barbie turned 50 in 2009, Mattel Inc. finally discovered the religion of color. For the first time, the pink color used in its distinctive logo is only one hue, PMS 219, a color to which the company now owns the rights. Prior to this change, there were over 15 different shades in use.

Yellow Tail took all of the complexity (and I would argue taste) out of wine by going to a simple color code. Yellow for chardonnay, purple for pinot noir, blue for cabernet merlot, and green for pinot grigio.

BARBARA ROBERTS

Barbara Roberts, a wordsmith and artist who needed a part-time job, applied for a position at Wal-Mart. Knowing the signature colors of the world's largest retailer, she donned a blue shirt/beige slacks outfit for her first interview. While you and I may not have paid attention to this subtlety, her prospective superiors and colleagues mentioned it at the beginning of every conversation. They applauded her effort at projecting the brand before she was even hired. Needless to say, she got the job!

The Crayola Box Effect

Binney & Smith, the makers of Crayola, understand the power of color. Since the introduction of its iconic 64-crayon box (with built-in sharpener!), it has added colors, removed colors, renamed colors, allowed consumers to vote for the new color and, in 2007, even unveiled an emotionally-tagged box. Awesome for orange, Best Friend for purple, and Happy Ever After for turquoise. Burnt Sienna was targeted for retirement, but a public outcry saved it from extinction. Trivia question: which color is the first to disappear from a box of crayons? (Answer: red).

Integrating Your Color

Recent studies show that color increases brand recognition by up to 80%; wow! You can reinforce your brand with color in a myriad of business ways:

- Pen ink (I use red)
- File folder
- Portfolio
- Mailing envelopes (makes a huge impact!)
- Wardrobe:
    Men: ties are a great opportunity
    Ladies: think of your purse
- Car
- Office paint color and décor
- Coffee mugs
- Premiums (pens, give-aways, etc.)
- Computer color (love the new Dell red!)
- Wallet, business card holder
- Cell phone/smart phone

YOUR TURN TO ACT

Take stock of your wardrobe. Look at your closet and check out any color trends. Since you are the brand, you should pick colors that already are near and dear to your heart.

Ask your Council. Poll your friends, colleagues, and family by phone (so they don't cheat and see what you're wearing!) and ask them to name one to three colors that symbolize you. See if they can give you a reason why.

Put responses to both your query and your closet on the same sheet of paper. Do you see any colors patterns?

Look at the *Psychology of Color* Chart in this chapter. Are your common colors consistent with your image that you want to protect? For example: if you are the queen of pink, you look good in pink, your wardrobe is predominantly pink, but you are a banker who typically deals with men, then this is a branding conflict. You might do better with green— the universal color of money.

Want to stay ahead of the color curve? Check out The Color Marketing Group to see its annual color forecasts: http://colormarketing.org/ (Hint: the hot color for 2010 is orange, also called mimosa).

Chapter 7

It's in the Cards
How to Create a Smokin' Business Card

STRIKE THE MATCH

OCCUPATION	BUSINESS CARD OPTIONS
1. Clothing retailer or fashion designer	A Film-type material/photo
2. Aluminum Siding or Building	B Aluminum
3. Copying, printing, or laminating	C Picture of your book
4. Tires	D Rubber
5. Cabinet Maker, wood worker	E Wood
6. Photographer	F Your Signature
7. Author	G Laminated
8. Handwriting Expert	H Fabric

The Business Card Is Paramount

If you're like most entrepreneurs, your business comes from personal interaction and communication. In other words, it is not TV ads or print ads that bring in the leads, but your personal efforts through contacts, networks, and referrals. Therefore, your business card is the most important part of your branding arsenal. And, if you are just setting up shop, it might be your only tool! More money and thought should be spent on this item than on your Web site, brochure, or case studies. Why? Because until you have favorably impressed prospects, they will never get beyond the first impression to see your brochure or Web site.

When I was pitching Coca-Cola to name their new water, I received a business card from a very senior marketing vice president. Was it flashy? No! Was it in its signature red? No! It was simple black type on a white background. Coke's efforts are all through mass advertising vehicles; the business card in their marketing world is irrelevant. But in our small-business world, it's critical!

Getting the Fundamentals Right

Although it might seem obvious, I can tell you from years of collecting thousands of business cards that approximately 25 percent don't work for a variety of reasons. When I traveled to Tucson for a huge speech, virtually none of the business cards that I received had an area code, because these entrepreneurs assumed they would only deal with people from Arizona!

WORDS of "*LIZ*DOM"

DON'T LET FORM OVERWHELM FUNCTION

Business cards are your most critical branding tool. Check to make sure that all type is readable and that your card can be scanned. Forego fancy lettering on new or unusual words to ensure that your message is received.

Or, how about business owners who only put their Web address rather than an e-mail address? I constantly hear that this move "drives visitors to my site." Wrong! It drives people away from you. You want it to be easy to do business with you. Making me first go to your Web site and then find a "contact us" link just to send you an e-mail exponentially increases your chance of being ignored. Given my Crackberry personality, I personally throw away all business cards without an e-mail address—to me, they are useless.

If gray is the new black in fashion, then 12-pt type is the new font size standard. If you have to put your glasses on to read your card, try again. With all of our computer work, our eyes are getting worse. No one will ever complain (except your designer) that your typeface is too readable.

BUSINESS CARD WARNING

If you find that acquaintances are continually writing on the back of your business card, take note. It is not a positive sign, but a negative one. Your business card should so clearly tell the reader about both you and your brand that no other communication is warranted.

Speaking of designers, they love to design artsy, interesting cards with script and new fonts. Use restraint. The card, of course, should reflect your brand, but don't let form overwhelm function.

In today's computer age, it's critical that your card can easily transfer via a card scanner. Before printing, conduct a test. Determine if the fields are populated correctly or that the card even scans.

Business Card Checklist

- Use 12-pt type or larger

- Test for card's "scan-ability"

- First Name and Last Name (both, unless you've become a one-name brand as discussed in Chapter 3)

- Title

- Company Name

- E-mail

- Web page

- Physical address: (optional)

- Second Side Copy

- Tagline (see Chapter 13 for all the details)

- Reflects your brand personality

- Consistent with your brand color

BRENT ALTOMARE

RED HOT *EXAMPLE*

Brent Altomare started Groovy Like a Movie, a video production house, in the year 2000 with four employees. He continued to grow and in 2007 moved into an enormous new facility with 15,000 square feet of space and thirteen employees. The new building is embellished with metallic details that this executive producer decided to incorporate into his business identity. Instead of simply using silver ink, he switched his entire card to a heavy metal card, almost like dog tags, with die-cuts. He's found that this upgrade has truly been his fire starter: it sparks conversation at every turn!

The Second Side

Business cards are inherently two-sided, meaning that precious real estate is going to waste if you leave the back side blank. This is your golden opportunity to sell.

As part of my new branding approach, I recommend that you never use the second side for your mission statement; those are internal messages that should simply be communicated through your actions to an external audience. Your goal is to live your brand, not tell me what you are trying to achieve.

On the back of its card, California Coast Credit Union offers free checks on your first printing. IBM (thank goodness) prints its customer support toll-free phone number on the back of all employees' cards, as inevitably a question will arise. Stanley Baquial, dentist, incorporates his Hawaiian heritage in his business card and the second side greets you with "aloha." Randy Greene of Make It Work, a computer support company, offers $25 off your first visit.

What can you include on your second side?

- Free marketing audit

- 20 percent off your first order

- Free glass of wine or appetizer at your restaurant

- Customer toll-free phone number

- Blog address

MONEY SAVING TIP *Try to work with a print broker instead of a particular printer directly. A print broker typically represents a number of printers, allowing him or her to find you the best price on printing essentials.*

Reflect Your Brand in Unusual Ways

This is your time to make a statement with your card. Based upon our earlier chapters on color and point of difference, you know that it must be consistent with your personality. I adore the business card of Michael Grant Hall, music and piano teacher. It is in the shape of a piano, and when you open it, notes from a sheet of music emerge. The restaurant, Crescent Heights Kitchen and Lounge, is adorned with buffed-to-a-shine walnut bars and fixtures. Its business card and marketing postcard reflect the grain of its signature wood immediately triggering a memory to your last visit.

MICHELLE BERGQUIST

RED HOT EXAMPLE

Michelle Bergquist used shape very effectively when she started the Corporate Basket in 1998 devoted to gift baskets as business gifts, thank-you mementos, and the like. Her business card was round. Everywhere she went, folks remembered it. When she sold the business in 1997 and started her new business, Michelle Bergquist, she retained the round shaped card. As we say, when there's smoke, there's fire!

YOUR TURN TO ACT

Before printing your card, test how well it scans by using a card scanner.

Print twenty cards on your home computer before printing in bulk. Distribute them as your new card and test the reaction. Are folks squinting? Are they asking you any questions about your contact information? Do they have to make notes on the back to understand your business? All of these responses hint towards a revision.

After distributing your test card, ask recipients to describe your brand. Check to ensure that the words are in tune with your brand's goals.

Chapter 8

Smoke Signals
How Phrases and Gestures Reinforce Your Brand

STRIKE THE MATCH

Pair the signature phrase with the celebrity

SIGNATURE PHRASE		CELEBRITY
1. "That's Hot!"	A	Meredith Vieira
2. "Yum-O!"	B	Emeril Lagasse
3. "How's That Working for Ya?"	C	Donald Trump
4. "You're Fired!"	D	Martha Stewart
5. "Is That Your Final Answer?"	E	Paris Hilton
6. "Shaken, Not Stirred"	F	Buzz Lightyear
7. "That's a Good Thing!"	G	Muhammad Ali
8. "Bam!"	H	Rachel Ray
9. "Float like a butterfly, sting like a bee"	I	Dr. Phil
10. "To Infinity and Beyond!"	J	James Bond

Signature phrases and gestures are great branding tools. As you can see from the above chart, if you can utter just one phrase and have instant recall, you are on your way towards a hot brand. Beyoncé is credited with bringing "bootylicious" into our vocabulary, and I bet that every single one of us has mimicked the Verizon dude on the commercials by asking on our cell phone, "Can you hear me now?"

Use a Signature Greeting

As we've learned so far, your brand doesn't necessary start with you; it begins with asking others and seeing how they remember you. With the "Your Turn to Act" section at the end of this chapter, I'll create steps to determine some trademark phrases and even how to invent your own. But from here, let's assume that you have a repertoire of words or phrases.

WORDS of "*LIZ*DOM"

USE SIGNATURES AS GREETINGS AND FAREWELLS

See if you can create a signature hello and goodbye. It can be as simple as "hola" or as casual as "yo." Of course, just make sure it's already a natural part of your speech.

Liz Goodgold

A good place to begin is with a greeting. I always think of Joey from Friends with his signature "how ya doin'?" Or Sly Stallone with his "Yo." These are not appropriate for me, but they work for them.

If you're a Southerner and it's not false or pretentious, you're welcome to use "y'all." On your next trip to Vegas, you might discover that at the Paris Hotel, you're always greeted with "bonjour." Francois Santore is a French professor at San Diego State University and a French textbook author. So, it's no surprise then that she also always answers her phone with a lively and lovely "bonjour." Oui, oui!

Comedians have built trademark expressions to an art form. Audience members can't wait to laugh with Steve Martin when he finally exclaims "excuse me!" Or John Pinette with his, "I say nay, nay." Or even Jeff Foxworthy with his "you might be a redneck if" jokes.

SANDRA LEE

Sandra Lee has made herself a household name through her successful cooking show on The Food Network, as well as through cookbooks and media appearances. What is most intriguing about her is the coining and employing of the word "semi-home-made." All of her cookbooks carry this moniker, she ends her cooking show with "make it best, make it simple, make it semi-homemade," and her official Web site is semihomeade.com, not Sandra Lee, further reinforcing her brand. A perfect way to cook up a hot brand!

Farewell Phrases

You can also use a farewell line. The MGM Grand reinforced its brand name by wishing its guests to "have a grand day."

I'll never forget my Italian intern, Francine Messori; she was a little dynamo, and her saying "ciao" at the end of every phone call always made me smile. Most importantly, every caller to my office remembered her and her signature phrase.

Two brothers who have heated up their branding efforts are Tom and Ray Magliozzi. You might know them better as Click and Clack, The Tappert Brothers on PBS radio for their Car Talk show. Drive over to their Web site and see how they make fun of themselves with caricatures, the "shameless commerce" navigational tab, or even links to "our lousy show." Their tongue-in-cheek style allows them to get away with ending every show with "don't drive my brother." This show is perfectly in tune.

Don't just think of these as suggestions to be used in person. Voice mail is the perfect place to integrate a signature greeting or farewell.

Reinforce Your Point of Difference

Sometimes you can substitute one little word to reinforce your point of difference. All of the hotel rooms at The Venetian in Las Vegas are suites, as reflected in all staff phrases such as "your suite is ready" or "you are in Suite 234." In fact, all literature in the room substitutes the word "suite." Just genius!

NORMA ANDRADE

Norma Andrade is very active in the Hispanic community, serving as President of the National Latina Women's Association as well as a financial planner. To reinforce her strength as an adviser who is fluent in Spanish, English, and the markets, she always has her voice mail greetings in both Spanish and English. En Fuego! (On Fire!)

RED HOT EXAMPLE

Use in Business Interaction

Every interaction is an opportunity to brand. In meetings, don't be afraid to use phrases that represent you. I used to get grief for constantly using the words "gobs" and "phenomenal," but now they are a trademark of all of my speeches. Even decibel levels can be brands…listen to Mary Murphy, the super-charged "So You Think You Can Dance" judge. If contestants make it on to her "hot tamale train," get ready for her ear-piercing and unforgettable scream.

Try to find ways to incorporate your personality even in your introductions to colleagues.

Use in Written Communication

And let's not forget the printed word. You can start or end your letters with your iconic phrase. Francine Allaire, founder of The Daring, concludes with "have a daring day." Apple Music signs off its letters with "your friend in music." "In good health" is a perfect closing for anyone in the health industry.

The two founders of The Wine Spies have taken their brand and woven it into every aspect of their business. Their e-mail letters start with "Covert Greetings." When you sign up for their daily wine specials, you are greeting with "Welcome Agent fill-in-the-blank." And, look for their wine deliveries to be labeled with "Top Secret Wine Shipment," or even "Top Secret Wine Gift Enclosed." Of course, their letters conclude with "Top Secret Regards."

Jet Blue cleverly calls its e-mail specials "Get Out of Town" and reinforces its own brand name.

Since your phrases reflect you, they give us a glimpse into your human side. Too often, lawyers, accountants, and financial planners feel that they must remain stiff and formal. As a result, their marketing messages all sound the same, with third-person-written-promises of accuracy and reliability. Yes, we want reliability, but a little personality too, please.

WORDS of "LIZDOM"

VEGAS, BABY!

Next time you're in sin city, look for all of the branding cues. Casino employees answer the phone "bonjour" at Paris, use the word "suite" instead of "room" at The Venetian, and wish you a "grand day" from the MGM Grand Hotel. Caesar's pumps music in from Cher, Elton John and Bette Midler to promote its shows. Luxor uses its distinctive pyramid shape throughout and even as door handles. Outfits are black, hot, tight, and sexy at The Palms and Hard Rock. And, don't overlook the scent wafting in from The Venetian. Sweet branding!

I urge you to integrate your brochure, Web site, and case studies with vivid examples of your brand; let it flourish! Here's a bold idea: put it on your license plate!

Gestures Count Too!

It's not only what you wear, but how you gesture that counts too. I'm a huge fan of Roger Ebert (may he be talking again soon) and he has a trademarked thumbs-up sign. Carol Burnett's ear-pulling signal is so trademark-worthy that the courts ruled in her favor after she sued the TV show Family Guy. The animated series argued that the cleaning lady was any old, generic one. But, ah ha! Since the cartoon character pulled her ear, it is trademark infringement! Remember from Chapter 4 that the source of goods is a goal of trademark law and in this case, it was clear that it was Carol Burnett.

YOUR TURN TO ACT

Review any audio or video recordings of you; I know it can be painful to watch or listen to yourself, but if it's easier, close your eyes and just listen to the words. See if you can find particular phrases or words that are "own-able."

Create a list of these phrases and then review with your Council.

Record a new voice mail greeting using at least one key word.

Chapter 9

Dress for Success

STRIKE THE MATCH

Pair the correct brand name with the wardrobe trait that made it famous:

WARDROBE TRAIT		BRAND NAME
1. Suspenders	A	Ellen DeGeneres
2. White Cowboy Hat	B	Alan Jackson
3. Black Mock Turtleneck	C	Minnie Pearl
4. Oversize Sunglasses	D	Popeye
5. Striped, Dolphin Shorts	E	Groucho Marx
6. Hat with a Price Tag	F	Senator Paul Simon
7. Always in Pants	G	Mr. Rogers
8. With a Cigar	H	Larry King
9. Red Bow Tie	I	Mort Sahl
10. Pipe	J	Richard Simmons
11. Button front sweater	K	Steve Jobs
12. V-neck sweater	L	Jackie O

Turn Up the Heat with a Trademarked Style

Just a few decades ago, everyone was trying to fit in, not stand out (myself included). Think back to your high school years and perhaps images of loafers, big skirts, Dittos, Members Only jackets, Candies, and Izod shirts were all the rage. You couldn't even go to school if you weren't wearing what everyone else was wearing. Blending in is the antithesis of branding.

But now you want to use your wardrobe to help identify you with your brand. We discussed wearing the color of your brand in Chapter 8. Here, we want to expand upon that dressing concept.

Some celebrities have literally made a name for themselves based upon how they dress. Shania Twain turned heads and boosted her status and sales when she belted out, "Man, I feel like a woman" at the GRAMMY Awards with gloves, short skirts, and thigh-high boots. She was emanating so much heat that even Nashville stars were unhappy with her for selling out to her sexiness. All I can say is that her track record speaks for itself. Sales went off the charts.

Jennifer Lopez skyrocketed into the tabloids with her Versace almost-there wrap dress. Wardrobe tape entered the nomenclature and her visibility (so to speak) was firmly established.

In 1994, Elizabeth Hurley walked the red carpet with Hugh Grant on her arm and not much else holding her dress together except a few strategically placed safety pins. That dress literally ignited her career, allowing her modeling and design business to explode.

And, sometimes you can literally wear your brand. At the 2008 Red Dress Awards, which honors women who make significant contributions in the fight against heart disease, Campbell's put its imprimatur on singer Toni Braxton. Her exquisite red dress had "M'mm! Good" printed all over it! When The Wall Street Journal launched its first ever magazine in the fall of 2008, its model also wore a dress made of its trademark printed prose.

Most women would know exactly what you mean if you described a classic Chanel outfit: tweed suit, short jacket, tons of gold necklaces and pearl ropes, all accented with a quilted lambskin bag. Tres chic!

Uniformly Good Idea

Before you start cringing on me, let me say that uniforms can work in branding. They influence perception from the get-go. Clinique was one of the first cosmetic companies to require that its salespeople wear a white lab coat. It does a great job of connecting the scientific, clinical approach to make-up with the brand. Do you remember when The Geek Squad first appeared on the scene? They made fun of themselves by wearing white shirts, pocket protectors, skinny black ties, and flood pants. They even named one of their services "Black Tie Protection," thereby further connecting with their imagery. Frangelica has a bottle in the shape of a friar that comes with a cassock belt. In commercials, to reinforce the connection, all of the actors are wearing the iconic rope belt.

WORDS of "*LIZ*DOM"

A FRESH LOOK AT UNIFORMS

Explore any type of trademark uniform that might fit with your brand. It could explain your profession, such as a chef's apron, lab coat, scrubs, or jogging suit.

Your uniform could be medical scrubs (works great

for anyone in health care), chef's toque (restaurant), or a tuxedo (wedding disc jockey). The host city of Athens paid homage to its roots during the 2004 Olympic Games by bestowing olive wreaths upon the heads of medal winners.

When Jason Tolin and Andrea Rustad show up to a networking event, they make an entrance! Wearing garb from the 1800s with top hat and coat or bustle skirts and gloves, they perfectly represent their brand: Ghostly Tours in History. If you call to make a scary appointment, listen to the haunting music while on hold—a brilliant representation of living the brand.

Rafael Nadal shot to the number-one ranking in tennis wearing a trademark muscle shirt (with real muscles included!), Capri pants, and a color-coordinated bandana. As part of his makeover to a more grown-up style, Nike was excited to have him unveil a more mature outfit with its signature swoosh on a shirt with sleeves, and shorts that ended above his knee. Then, moments before his first 2008 US Open appearance, Rafa (as he is fondly known) reneged, stating that he wasn't ready to change quite yet. Winning Wimbledon, the Olympic gold medal, and The French Open for the fourth consecutive time in one year just made him too reluctant to change his style that year.

Dressing to Improve Your Brand Image

Sometimes in business, you are what you wear. Have you ever noticed that wearing your favorite and expensive suit just seems to make everything go your way? Christina Binkley, reporter for The Wall Street Journal swears by her St. John suit. Magically, she's transformed into a VIP: maitre d's snap to attention, she receives special consideration, and retail salespeople are tripping over themselves to help her. Perhaps Julia Robert's character in Pretty Woman was right when she too noticed that she is snubbed in high-end Beverly Hills stores while dressed as a prostitute, but fawned over when she is transformed (thanks to Richard Gere's dollars) into a well-to-do lady.

K.L. Moore, an image expert consultant, notes that your ultimate success may be determined by the image you project. Countless studies affirm that individuals with a strong visual brand make more money, attract more clients, are hired quicker, promoted faster, and receive preferential treatment. How to join this elite group? Here are her top three strategies for dressing success:

> 1. **Use the One-Notch Rule**. Always dress one notch above your clients, peers, and competitors. If your client will be "casual," you should show up in "business casual." If the dress standard at work is "business casual," you should wear "business appropriate." Remember, you are "The Expert."

> 2. **Tailor Your Visual Message**. Certain clothing details can make you look more authoritative or more approachable. Adding collars, cuffs, and lapels increases your authority, while the lack of those elements can make you appear more approachable. Weigh your options carefully.

> 3. **Focus on Cost Per Wearing (CPW)**. Instead of looking for the "sale" signs throughout a store, focus on your "needs" list. Look for quality-made, investment pieces that project your right image. Yes, it may initially cost a handsome sum, but on a cost per wearing scale, it might turn out to be the best purchase you've ever made!

INDRA NOOYI

At age 52, Indra Nooyi is the CEO of PepsiCo, number 63 on Fortune Magazine's Top 500 List. Born in India, mother of two daughters, and a vegetarian, some might think her an unlikely candidate to be at the reins of the world's largest snack maker. But long before she took that position, she created her own strong brand by speaking out against obesity and other issues. Today she champions "Performance with a Purpose" to help make healthier foods, leave a smaller carbon imprint on the world, and take care of the workforce. Her fashion style is distinctive as well: impeccably dressed, but with always an Indian fashion accessory, such as a richly colored silk scarf across her pinstriped suit.

Accessory after the Fact

Perhaps dressing for your brand will be easier if you focus on just an accessory, not an entire ensemble. For men, signature ties work well. From my home state of Illinois, the late Senator Paul Simon always wore a red bow tie. Even if you couldn't find many members of Congress, he was easy to recognize.

Many ladies opt for pins that signify their occupation. I've seen great dangling chef tools as label pins; purse attachments that are a dollar sign (financial planner), and pink purses (Mary Kay). The point is that you should seek out something that works for you.

At the MAGIC trade show recently, I met Leanna Harrison, one of the founders of Strapilicious: handmade, artsy bra straps with beads intended to peek out from women's clothes. It's a great idea that's attached itself to the booming free-form idea of bras that become a fashion statement. And, what are all of the women wearing at their booth? Their products, of course!

pablo solomon

A.A. Solomon was an artist struggling with his career—in part, because he didn't look the part! After a name change to pablo solomon (all lower case, please), a wardrobe makeover, and even an earring, he now fits the image of an artist. His new brand has landed him promotions with PBS for Art 21 and inclusion in Joyce Schwarz's book The Vision Board. This is a stroke of genius!

Dress the Part

Certain occupations demand that you flaunt your brand. If you are a hairdresser, I expect not a hair to be out of place. If you're in the jewelry business like my friend TC Leary, you should be as well adorned as she is. If you are an optometrist, have fun with fashion frames. You should have an entire wardrobe of fun frames to show how they are always in style. The same goes for those selling clothing. Lil' Kim wears a huge bling necklace that spells out her name.

Elizabeth Gordon, best-selling author of *The Chic Entrepreneur: Put Your Business in Higher Heels*, has woven her brand into her dress with apparently enough shoes to rival Imelda Marcos and with a chic fashion bent to boot!

Kristen Caldwell is a representative for Silpada, the silver jewelry multi-level marketing company. At every function, she is a walking showcase of how good the jewelry looks. What a shining example!

TRACEY DOWNEY-RACEN

Tracey Downey is the mastermind behind the unctuous, fabulous chocolates at Downey's Chocolates. Starting her business in December 2005 with revenues of $298.00, her 2006 revenues exceed $600,000 and today she is en route to $1 million in revenue. Donning a periwinkle chef's coat at every networking event, she credits her garb as getting the attention she needs to explain her Signature Gourmet, Big Mouth, and Vegan chocolates. Her products are now available at Whole Foods, her original location in Laguna Niguel, and on-line. Her brand is on fire.

RED HOT EXAMPLE

The Spectacle of Spectacles

Glasses are an entire category unto themselves. Look at the list below, and I bet that just from the personality alone you could guess what the glasses look like:

- Harry Potter
- Elton John
- Twitch

- John Lennon
- Jackie O
- Bono

- Mr. Peepers
- Liz Claiborne

Hats On and Off

Hats also remain a dress of distinction. Alan Jackson has the white cowboy hat, whereby it seems that every other country singer has opted for the ubiquitous black hat. Those of us who revere wine instantly recognize Mike Grgrich with his trademark black beret. Younger viewers count on Jamie Hyneman with his beret to separate fact from fiction in the top-rated Mythbusters TV series on the Discovery Channel. Bella Abzug earned a place in politics not only for her views, but also for her big hats as well. A hat completes the ensemble for Boy George, Indiana Jones, and even Cedric the Entertainer.

I, of course, would be remiss not to mention the Red Hat Society, a group of women aged 50 and up who are passionate in their pursuit of fun, friendship, freedom, and fulfillment. These ladies enter a room with their purple outfits, outrageous red hats, and fun is sure to follow! Founder Sue Ellen Cooper took a poem by Jenny Joseph and turned it into an organization that now boasts 30,000 chapters in all 50 states. Whoa!

The Shape of Things to Come

At first blush, it might seem unusual to brand by body part, but of course it is part of your brand. In fact, most celebrity contracts include clauses about image as a legal requirement. For example, Wilford Brimley was limited to only losing/gaining ten pounds when he was the Quaker Oats spokesman. And, most model requirements also have maximum weight limits.

Scott Ogilvie is the wizard behind this book cover and all of my Web sites and logos. As head of Ogilart, he designs, illustrates, and makes magic out of images. When he steps out behind the computer, he's not hard to find as he towers over six feet tall with striking strawberry blonde hair.

Shape is a great branding tool. Apple just received a patent on the signature shape of its I-Pod. Toblerone candy has a triangular package to represent the Matterhorn—the mountains, not the Disneyland ride! The triangular shape also works for the Luxor in Vegas. And Valium was one of the first die-cut drugs with the letter "V." Many women would recognize the puffy, quilted shape of a Chanel handbag. Its greatest branding trick, however, is duplicating that shape and pattern into all of its other products, even including eye shadow!

A brilliant ad is currently running by Sharpie. It simply shows a golf ball transformed into a soccer ball by virtue of a few strategic swipes of Sharpie's trademark black marker. The voice-over then declares that it is the only pen worthy of soccer star, David Beckham. Sharpie scores a GOOOOOOOOOOOOOOOOOOOOOOOOAL!!!

Richard Branson tried Virgin Cola in the shape of a woman, but the product failed regardless. The female form, however, works very well for John Paul Gaultier. This designer, known for creating Madonna's cone-shaped bustier, introduced special edition bottles every year and they all come packaged in a can!

Voss has the classiest bottle of all—just a long, tall, bottle like a literal drink of water. I'm also fond of the curved neck of Frequensea. And here's one that sums up shape perfectly: Pepperidge Farm Milano Cookies. The dark chocolate center and luscious vanilla cookie is shaped into a man and woman holding each other. The headline: "Bold dark chocolate. Light golden cookie. Soulmates." Yummy on all counts!

YOUR TURN TO ACT

Discover if consumers have a trademark idea of how you should dress. If you really are a tech guy, you might have fun with it and intentionally wear a pocket protector.

See if glasses can work for you, even without prescription lenses. Twitch, one of the finalists from a season of *"So You Think You Can Dance"*, doesn't even need glasses, but wears clear glass lenses anyway as his signature trait.

Chapter 10

Spice Up the Silence
Using Music and Voice as Mnemonic Devices

Pair the correct brand name with the celebrity who does the voice-over commercial:

BRAND CELEBRITY	VOICE	
1. Kaiser Permanente	A	Peri Gilpin
2. CNN	B	Gene Hackman
3. AOL	C	James Earl Jones
4. Stouffers	D	Susan Sarandon
5. Wells Fargo	E	Allison Janney
6. BMW	F	Morgan Freeman
7. Crestor	G	Mandy Patinkin
8. Lowe's Home Improvement	H	Julia Roberts
9. Visa	I	Patricia Clarkson

Music Influences Our Mood

Sound and music are great influencers. They are directly tied to our mood. Want to perk up? Put on The Rolling Stones. Want to wallow in your sorrow? Try Joni Mitchell. Ready for a romantic evening? There's always Barry White. Your friend at the gym was right: putting on energetic music really does energize you.

WORDS of "*LIZ*DOM"

MUSIC

Explore any type of trademark music that might fit with your brand. Transcriber or wordsmith? Try "Gonna Sit Right Down and Write Myself a Letter." Perhaps a travel agent? Try "Red Sails in the Sunset"! Sell whirlpool baths? Try "Tiny Bubbles"!

SUDS

Make Music

Since music influences mood, you need to find ways to integrate it into your brand. If you have an office, then piping in music is an easy fix. Of course, ensure that the music is appropriate for your brand, as well as the noise level. Good retailers, such as Neiman Marcus, have zoned their music so it's appropriate to each department. Next time you're in a store, wander from the teen's department to the men's department and listen for a discernable difference in the music choice. The last time I was in Abercrombie & Fitch, for example, the music was so loud that I clearly knew this music wasn't intended for me, but for the younger, hipper customers.

Studies are clear that all music, regardless of type, more positively influences the experience than no music. Aesthetician Tina Montgomery personally selects music without drums to ensure her clients get a restful experience during their facials. In essence, the sounds of silence do not help your cause. Anyone in the health care field, especially dentists, should aim for soothing, calming sounds. A recent Temple University study revealed that people who listened to music during a colonoscopy required less sedation than those who didn't listen.

The pace of the music is also important. Not surprisingly, the faster the music, the faster the visitors will move in and out of your office, store, or restaurant. Again, check out the tunes the next time you're in your favorite fast-food joint and note the fast tunes. They want you in and they want you out—quickly! But, if you want folks to linger, slow music is the way to go. And, most of us know this fact: the longer you are in a retail place, the more you will be likely to buy. This is a key reason why Barnes & Noble, Nordstrom, and other retailers have set up cafes. They want you to stay as long as possible.

A study recently demonstrated that in a restaurant where French music was played, sales of French wines increased. The study was also replicated with German music, resulting in an increase in the sale of German wines.

United Airlines has successfully linked its brand with Gershwin's "rhapsody in blue." Metropolitan Life adopted the Peanut's theme song for its commercials. Unfortunately, Tide just started using this music too—a bad branding move because it instantly reminded me of Met Life.

Using Distinctive Tones

Other sounds, such as tones, also can be used to create your signature brand. The Olympic moment starts for me the minute I hear the first two notes of that emotional sound. Even saying the brand name, Ricola, makes me sing it, just as I've heard hundreds of times from its TV commercials. NBC has the oldest audio trademark for its ding, ding, ding, a point that is nicely driven home by the advertising slogan of "chime in." Harley Davidson tried to get a trademark on its kick-start sound, but failed. Most of us can recognize, for bad or for worse, Microsoft's Windows start-up sound, or even Intel's tone. Verizon's ring is distinctive, as is Motorola's. They are, that is, if you haven't downloaded a cooler, hipper ring tone. Of course, my perennial favorite is the opening notes from *Sex and The City.*

The Power of Your Voice

Close your eyes and imagine what the CNN announcer would sound like if it were Fran Drescher instead of James Earl Jones. Or, pretend to be Robin Leach of *Lifestyles of the Rich and Famous.* Or, think of Sean Connery without that Scottish lilt. These voices are distinctive; these voices are part of their brand.

So, how can you use sound to help your brand? Well, the easy version starts with your voice. You can't change your voice, but you can change your speaking pattern, cadence, tone, and pacing, which all influence how your message is perceived and received.

Voice exercises are recommended before any public speaking. Try tongue twisters such as "she sells sea shells along the sea shore," as well as lip and jaw exercises to loosen up the mouth.

WORDS of "*LIZ*DOM"

THE POWER OF YOUR VOICE

It's true: it's not what you say, but how you say it that influences perception. Review your pacing, tone, umms, aahs, public stance, or anything that takes away from your message. If needed, hire a vocal coach for even one session.

SUDS

And, according to Susan Berkley, CEO of The Great Voice Company in Englewood Cliffs, New Jersey, we have just seven seconds to make an impression. The voice is divided into two components: verbal and vocal. Verbal is what we say; vocal is how we say it. To improve your vocal skills, Berkley recommends these tips:

- **Improve Your Elocution**—In other words, speak clearly and succinctly. Pronounce every consonant and vowel. If you're not speaking clearly, you're not retaining your listener's attention.

- **Slow Down**—If you're speaking too fast, you're losing your chance to connect. Don't be afraid to pause and let your message sink in.

- **Find Your Perfect Pitch**—When you're speaking in your optimal pitch, your voice is at the height of its resonance. To find your perfect pitch, hum a few bars of a favorite song. That pitch is probably where your voice is at its healthiest.

- **Use a Tape Recorder**—Hearing yourself can help you identify the "ums" and "uhs" in your speech as well as unnatural pitches, tones and pronunciation mistakes.

DON LAFONTAINE

Known as the Voice of God, with more than 5,000 movie trailers to his credit and finally his own GEICO commercial, Don LaFontaine was the man who seemed to start every voice-over with an ominous "in a world where there is no hope." He truly revolutionized the movie industry with his innovative production company in 1964, dedicated to creating movie trailer advertisements. Virtually all movie promotion before that time was relegated to newspaper ads. He died in September 2008, with all of us wishing his fire had burned a little longer.

How to use music if you're a home-based business? There's always voice mail. You can use it before or after the dreaded beep, or even as light background music. Music emanating from your Web site is also an option. I use music to set the mood before my speeches (gotta love *"Burning Down the House"* by The Talking Heads).

GARRY RIDGE

Garry Ridge has been at the helm as CEO and President of WD-40 for over ten years. He's also the author, with Ken Blanchard, of Helping People Win at Work: A business Philosophy Called Don't Mark my Paper—Help Me Get an A. But, one of Garry's greatest strengths is his thick Australian accent. He uses it as his excuse to ask questions and admit he doesn't know the answer. Even being in the US for years hasn't tempered his signature cadence, his Aussie slang, or even his signature "g'day" greeting. Bloody good show!

RED HOT EXAMPLE

Duffy Fainer has definitely got "the voice." He works as an announcer, master of ceremonies, voice-over artist, and even a game show host. The minute you land on his site, of course, you hear that mellifluous tone. Even his Web site notes his gift by being called "Voice by Duffy."

Look for every opportunity to use music in your business: on-hold music, in your office, in your store, in promotional material, etc.

Work with your voice—the next public speaking event, even if at a meeting, have someone give you a "no holds barred" review of how you did. Did you stutter? Insert too many "umms"? Did you stand nervously? Practice using your voice to its best advantage.

Determine your unique aural qualities, whether it is a second language, strong accent, etc. Make sure to record voice mail greetings that distinguish you.

Chapter 11

Feel the Heat
Using All Senses to Trigger Recall

STRIKE THE MATCH

Scent Trivia Quiz?

What's the world's best-selling perfume?

What's a man's favorite scent?

Are men or women more likely to have a better nose?

What percent of communication is scent-based?

What scent is considered "old lady"?

Which scent can lift your mood?

Smell Is the Closest Link to Memory

Less than 2 percent of all marketing messages are communicated via the sense of smell, yet scent provides the closest links to memories. Studies show that a man's favorite scent is food: vanilla, chocolate, and any other baking smell tops their list. Older folks (65+) often remember fondly the smells of freshly cut grass, eucalyptus trees, or other natural smells. My generation tends to like all of the artificial smells, such as that new car smell, new shower curtain smell, etc.

WORDS of "*LIZ*DOM"

THE SENSE OF SMELL IS UNDERUSED

Less than 2 percent of all marketing messages are communicated via the sense of smell, yet scent provides the closest links to memories. Find ways to connect to your customer via this sense and you can create an indelible impression.

Creating Signature Scents

You can build a positive connection between your brand and a smell by creating a signature scent. Crayola Crayons has actually trademarked its smell. Omni Hotels puts eucalyptus scent in all of its showers to create a clean, aromatic experience. Limited Brands created a proprietary smell of orange and ginger for the Marriott hotel chain. And Westin Hotels & Resorts has created a signature White Tea Scent to spritz in its lobbies, corridors, and other public places.

Sheraton Hotels & Resorts came up with a lovely idea that was both aromatic and visually captivating - placing one dozen yellow roses in the lobby of every one of its hotels. After six months, the parent corporation pulled the plug, stating that the roses were simply too costly. This type of thinking is sadly short sighted, ultimately resulting in no long-term payoff. The hotel should have kept the concept for at least a year. Again, consistency is the secret to solid branding.

Early on in my career, I tried to sell Howard Schultz, CEO of Starbucks, on the ease and profit opportunity of easy-bake scones. He dismissed the idea, noting that his stores would and should always smell like coffee. He quipped that if he baked on premises, "my stores would smell like a Cinnabon." Of course, there's been a roller-coaster effect here as the ubiquitous coffee chain brought in breakfast sandwiches, which to me made the place smell like Burger King. In early 2008, when Mr. Schultz again resumed the helm, he boasted to the press that one of the first things to change would be the elimination of the cheese breakfast entrees. Then, in late summer of 2008, breakfast was again back on the menu, due to the struggling profits and sales issues as the chain explores how to create a better cooking option with lower olfactory emissions!

Scent Influences Mood

Smell can actually alter mood. Citrus is known to put folks in a happy mood. Peppermint can perk you up, and cinnamon improves vigor and concentration. A recent study also found that subjects exposed to the scent of ylang-ylang saw their blood pressure drop almost instantly.

Americans are literally buying into the home fragrance market, as sales of air fresheners totaled $2.05 billion in 2007—up a whopping 543 percent from 2002!

MONEY SAVING TIP *Instead of buying fresh flowers weekly, opt for scented candles that add ambience and scent at the same time. It can become a surprisingly nice touch in a traditional office environment.*

MANDY AFTEL

Mandy Aftel embraces branding with the sense of smell by formalizing it into a business. With a consultation fee starting at $2500, she helps businesses to create a signature scent. Now, that smells like sweet success to me!

RED HOT
EXAMPLE

KUMHO holds the dubious distinction for introducing the world's first aromatic tire. Yeah! I was worried that my tires simply smelled like black rubber, but now I can special order tires that smell like lavender, orange, or jasmine for my Mercedes—be still my heart! The problem here is that this is not an area appropriate for branding. In very short order, your tires will smell like the road. Further, they are outside of the car, beyond the area where it will influence mood or perception.

Using Sense of Smell in Advertising

Bloomingdales, in 2007, boldly emitted the aroma of the Donna Karan DKNY Delicious Night onto surrounding sidewalks to celebrate the fragrance launch. The TV show, Weeds, took out scratch n' sniff ads with the smell of the evil weed to pique interest. And, Kraft Foods created scent-laden cards with the smell of its new DiGiorno Garlic Bread Pizza.

The streets of London had one of the first scented bus shelters. Pedestrians could push a button to get a whiff of the new Procter & Gamble's Head & Shoulders Citrus Fresh shampoo. The consumer products giant also scored a coup with its Ivory Lavender in 2006. It sponsored a Rose Bowl float to introduce this brand extension. Besides reaching an estimated 50 million viewers (that's right), it spewed from the float the calming smell of the product.

Smell Increases Value, Perception, and Sales

Avon sees a positive return on its investment when it purchases scent-strips of fragrances in magazine ads. A spokeswoman says that it directly ties into capturing new customers and bumping sales.

In a test conducted for Nike, two identical pairs of running shoes were placed in two identical rooms except for the aroma (No! Not of running shoes). One room had a floral scent, and the other had no scent. By an overwhelming margin of 84 percent, testers preferred the shoes from the fragrant room. But get this: the estimated value of the shoes was over $10 higher than the non-scented room.

Lunn Poly, a UK travel firm, saw a bump in sales when it pumped the smell of coconut into its stores. You might do well to scent your car—subtly, especially if you are a real estate agent or any other professional who frequently has passengers.

Many visitors to Las Vegas' Venetian Hotel and Casino have experienced its distinctive aroma. The company behind this signature smell is AromaSys, which bills itself as the "premier provider of custom-scented environments for resorts, casinos, elite hotels and spa properties in North America." Many visitors to these establishments comment favorably and enjoy the "feel good" fragrances. On the flip side however, some people dislike the smells, even to the point of claiming that it causes them breathing problems. So, if you think about claiming a scent that will reinforce your brand, weigh the pros and cons, and choose wisely!

Tastefully Yours

We all know that taste can be such a delightful addition. In fact, studies show that if I have any food or beverage during my meeting with you, I will rate the meeting more positively than if I had nothing to eat or drink at all. What this research demonstrates is the power of using all of the senses in your branding. Adding smell, taste, visual communication, or music makes the experiences more positive and lasting.

I am literally licking my chops thinking about the marketing opportunities offered by the new lick and taste samples in magazines. Welch's kicked off the tongue-a-thon with a chance to try its 100 percent grape juice in People magazine. It's highly controversial, and some might even argue "gross," but I believe that trying is buying. Once you get the taste in someone's mouth, you have the opportunity to sell.

DOUBLETREE HOTELS

If you are a road warrior, perhaps you begin to salivate the minute you get close to the front desk at a Doubletree Hotel. Why? You know that upon check-in, you'll be greeted with warm, chocolate chip cookies. Each day, the hotel chain distributes over 29,000 cookies. Started in the late 1980s, this treat heats up your sense of smell, your stomach, and makes you feel a little more connected to Doubletree. A very sweet idea!

Your Tactile Sense—The Forgotten Feeling

It's easy to forget the sense of touch, but not its power; after all, the skin is the largest organ of the body. Note that even in our language, we say, "you are touched by me," or that movie "touched you." We even teach our children the power of touch with the classic *Pat the Bunny*. On every page, toddlers place a finger through the book to touch the hair of the bunny, the rough skin of an elephant, or the silkiness of a blanket. In business, you can make touch work for you.

I love business cards that feel fabulous. I intentionally have my business cards made super thick, almost like a book cover. Why? It subtly communicates that the card is strong and reliable and I am too; I am here today and will be there tomorrow. Raised ink, die-cuts, super smooth paper and unusual material also work on a business card to set your tactile senses ablaze!

One of my favorite wines is referred to as the Marilyn Merlot velvet bottle. The label is velvet and just aches for you to caress her. Iron Stone Bank has huge signage in front of their offices that are, of course, iron and stone. Even from afar, the rough edges of these materials reflect the brand. Clearly, much time and engineering has gone into creating the controls for gamers' platforms, including the X-box and the Wii. They must feel right. In fact, it often feels to us of the baby boomer generation that our children have amazing finger dexterity due to their constant thumbing, instant messaging, typing, texting, and mousing.

YOUR TURN TO ACT

Determine all of the places you can use a signature scent; investigate employing your signature one throughout.

Explore even simple fragrant boosters, such as fresh flowers every Monday in an office environment.

Look for innovative ways to use the sense of touch—on business cards, on office furniture, even on business report covers.

Chapter 12

The Head Whip Effect
How to Create a Network and Infomercial Bonfire!

STRIKE THE MATCH

Pair the correct brand name with the its key phrase:

BRAND NAME

KEY PHRASE

1. Plop, plop, fizz, fizz
2. Takes a licking and keeps on ticking
3. Where's the beef?
4. Whassup?
5. Where the turf meets the surf
6. Zoom, zoom, zoom
7. Snap, crackle, pop!
8. Good to the last drop
9. Can you hear me now?
10. Mmmm, Mmmmm good!
11. Wring around the collar

A Campbell's
B Timex
C Alka Seltzer
D Del Mar Race Track
E Maxwell House
F Wendy's
G Budweiser
H Wisk
I Rice Krispies
J Verizon
K Mazda

The Myth of the 30-Second Infomercial

Fugetaboutit —as Tony Soprano would say. The 30-second infomercial is no longer a reality. In the past, it was believed that if you and a potential customer were trapped in an elevator (ha!), you could deliver an advertising spiel guaranteed to impress and close the deal. No!

Just as watching the entire 30-seconds of a commercial has become unusual, the same has happened with a long infomercial. We do not want commercials blasting at us for 30 seconds at a time. Instead, we skip the ads thanks to TiVo and digital video recorders. But, statistics show that we will interact with the brand if it engages us. Hence, Internet-linked commercials that allow us to vote online, as successfully happened with the Frito-Lay commercials in 2008 and 2007 or the contest that allowed a new songwriter to perform with Justin Timberlake at the 2008 GRAMMY'S.

Advertising today is a dialogue of two-way communication. On the Web, we rant about our opinion and write our own reviews on Amazon. The smart companies respond.

What has happened with the big brands also happens with our own personal brand; we do not have permission to speak uninterrupted for thirty seconds. It's now a dance. I say an intriguing first sentence and bam! It should interest you to such an extent that you respond with "Oh, tell me more." Now, you have permission to fan the flame and speak a little longer.

WORDS of "*LIZ*DOM"

WE ALL HAVE ADD (ATTENTION DEFICIT DISORDER)

In today's fast-paced world, it's important to note that we no longer have a 30-second time span to drone on about ourselves—we have seven seconds. Make every one count!

Welcome to the 7-Second Hook

If the 30-second infomercial is over, it's time to usher in the 7-second hook. It's your attention "getter." It's your "It was a pleasure to burn" first sentence of a book as captivating as Ray Bradbury's in *Fahrenheit 451*.

The 7-second hook is critical because it is your first impression, your initial spark. I believe it is analogous to putting a home up for sale—your first offer is usually your best offer. There are many reasons, but I believe the key one is the "new" factor. Our first reactions to new items or people are formed in just a few seconds. Today, you can still use "new" for products and even publicity appearances.

I have created hundreds of these introductions for entrepreneurs, so here are a few suggestions:

- **Hit Them with the Unexpected**—A structural engineer starts with "I hold up banks...and gyms, houses, and all sorts of other structures." TLC Shipping former owner Tess Bockes told people that she "shipped the outrageous."

- **Try for Humor**—A little laughter always works as an ice breaker. Speaker Sarita Maybin introduces herself as "helping your employees play nicely in the sandbox together." I heard a dentist recently say that he "works for the tooth, the whole tooth, and nothing but the tooth!" Ken Morrison, District Director for the US Department of Labor's Wage and Hour District Office in San Diego, recognizes the layers of government and says that "government is a many splintered thing."

- **Mnemonic Devices**—George James uses a rhyme to increase recall: "George James; he entertains!" Love it!

- **Double Meanings**—Jackie Beveridge, who has an automobile repair business, always looks surprised when she says, "Oh, have we met? Perhaps it was by accident." Laser Eye Center employees announce that "if you're ready to get rid of your glasses, they're the ones to see." Mortgage expert Julie Otto simply states that if you're looking for a loan, you "otto know me."

- **Keep It Simple**—Patent lawyer Greg Einhorn works on tremendously complicated scientific patent issues, but introduces himself simply with, "I help people with their inventions."

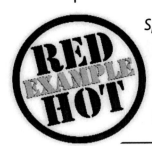

JILL LESLY JONES

Speaking Coach Jill Lesly Jones simply tells listeners that she helps people speak "gooder." That slice of humor always begins the conversation on a bright note.

How to Use Your Hook

This is your time to use it—when meeting new people. Scott Ginsberg proudly wears a nametag at all times and has even dubbed himself "The Guy with the Nametag." So, even as he is introducing himself, you're visually learning his name. Great trick!

The Reality of Networking

Too many entrepreneurs have the errant idea that networking is meeting as many people as possible and then soliciting business. Wrong! Networking is a chance to listen, to learn, and to help someone else. Your goal is to learn as much as possible about someone so that you can add value to his or her network. You must give, not take, and then witness all of the rewards that come back to you.

No, this is not an altruistic speech, but a reality of today's marketplace. You cannot attend events with the ultimate goal of nabbing someone to sign your purchase order. Instead, your goal must be to determine who might be able to refer business to you, who has the same target market, and then begin to develop a relationship. And remember, networking is a lifestyle; it is not a specific-goal oriented action to get you a new job or client.

ROBBIE MOTTER

RED HOT EXAMPLE

If you are a woman who does business in California, I guarantee you know Robbie Motter. Leaving corporate America behind in 1985, she vowed to pursue a path that enabled her to connect people to others who would help them pursue their dreams. Today, she is a gold founding sponsor of For You Network, a not-for-profit company founded to empower women. She is also a Western and Mid-Atlantic Regional Coordinator for the National Association of Female Executives (over 66,000 members strong), and she is the head of her own marketing and public relations company called (no surprise here) Contacts Unlimited. Her personal motto is "it's all about 'showing up.'" You will find Robbie at hundreds of events each year. If so, go ahead and introduce yourself, and she'll undoubtedly have a connection for ya!

Secrets for Maximizing Your Networking Time

Having attended hundreds of networking events over my entrepreneurial career, I have learned how to turn these brief interactions into long-lasting business relationships. Here are my top eleven secrets:

1. Eat Beforehand—Virtually none of us look good trying to stand, balance a glass of wine in one hand, eat with the other, and make a favorable impression. So, my number-one networking rule is NO EATING! If the event starts at 5 p.m., you can guarantee that I will be having a hearty snack at 4 p.m. Networking is not a tasting festival; it's a meeting festival.

2. Dress Appropriately—As we discussed in Chapter 8, this is your golden opportunity to showcase your brand via your clothes, style, color, and accessories. But, your feet also deserve consideration. Ladies, you know what I'm talking about here. If your four-inch Jimmy Choos match the outfit, but kill your feet, pick another pair that you can stand in painlessly for hours. Sitting on the sidelines simply won't do.

3. Linger—Great networkers arrive early and leave late. They don't schedule meetings that could run late before the event or plan commitments immediately afterward. Being first to check in has two major advantages: first, no lines, no waiting! Second, you have the chance to scan a display table full of nametags—a perfect way to determine who will be attending. You can then focus your efforts accordingly.

4. Go with a Goal in Mind—For example, let's say that you are interested in meeting someone from Dial Corporation because they are headquartered in your home city of Phoenix. Your focus, therefore, is to find Dial personnel. You then accomplish this goal by asking all of the folks that you do know at the event, including members of the organizing group, to help you find the attending Dial employees.

5. Moderation—My rule is one glass of wine and I always keep it in my left hand. Why? To allow for easy shaking of my right hand to meet new people.

6. Pre-Plan the Business Card Issue—The deadly sin of networking is running out of business cards. So, always keep a few in your wallet, an extra box in the car, and a business card case loaded. And, I recommend that you wear a blazer, jacket, or pants that have easy access pockets for your business card. Again, it's hard to look professional if you are digging through your purse or wallet to find your card. And, here's a tip to forever avoid giving out someone else's business card: Left pocket is for your business cards; right pocket is for the business cards you receive. Shake with the right hand; give your business card with the left. Perfect every time!

7. Make Eye Contact—The person you are meeting with at that moment in time is the most important person there—period. No looking around with the hope of finding someone else more interesting. Stay in the moment and then move on. You will be respected and rewarded.

8. Listen—Really listen. Studies show we only use 25 percent of our listening ability. Concentrate, ask questions, and take the time to truly learn something about your new acquaintance.

9. Name Tag—Ideally, you should have a professionally printed name tag rather than the peel n' stick variety. Regardless of the variety, always place your name tag on your right side. Why? Because when you shake hands it pushes your right shoulder forward, reinforcing your verbal introduction with your written name.

10. Do Something for Someone Else First—In every interaction, try to discover your acquaintance's ideal target market, the problem they are currently facing, or if they are looking for a vendor. I have helped so many people find

jobs (and it is not my job!) just by connecting people. It will always come back.

11. Follow-Up—My favorite "F" word. Every interaction requires scanning the business cards you received into your database and any follow-up you mentioned that you would send. I try to use the 24-hour rule. Every stitch of follow-up is completed within one day. Your follow-up can simply be a two-sentence note, the forwarding of your e-newsletter, or an invitation to meet for lunch.

MONEY SAVING TIP *Do your networking follow-up over coffee instead of lunch; you'll find that by meeting at a coffee place such as Starbucks, your guest will seldom order any food, meaning your entire investment might be less than $5. And, you don't have to worry about how to talk and eat at the same time.*

12. Act Like the Host—Keep your eyes open for wallflowers; take the initiative of introducing attendees to each other. They will feel more welcome, and you've found a way to meet new people by adding value to the event.

13. Be Current on the News—Even if you are not a Yankees fan, Michael Jordan wannabe, or news junkie, then this is the time to quickly review CNN.com or USA Today to ensure that you can smoothly schmooze your way

through the event. Finding a common ground is the first
step towards building a relationship.

14. **Introduce Yourself Twice**—"Bond, James Bond." Or "Forest. Forrest
Gump" Both of these imaginary characters do a great job of helping
us remember their names. Another trick towards flawless recall is to
employ some sort of device upon introducing yourself. Gregg Ward,
for example, always says "Gregg: it has three g's." My late colleague
John Mizhir always introduced himself as "rhymes with leisure."
Nancy Chetron introduces herself as "chevron with a T." Lon Wood
laughs and says, "yes, like the grass." Writer/editor Theresa Jache
(pronounced yaki) has too much fun with her name by introducing
herself with "my friends call me Teri, Teri Yaki. Get it?"

Join a Leads Group

If you want to network where the overriding goal really is business building and referrals, join a specific leads group. There is Le Tip, BNI, Leads
Club, RBN, and TeamWomen, just to name a few. Many Chambers of
Commerce, associations, and organizations have also set up specialized
leads groups. The rules typically include allowing only one professional
per industry attending mandatory meetings and becoming an active referral source. Many successful executives today credit their early success to
these types of groups.

WORDS of "*LIZ*DOM"

NETWORKING

People do business with people they know, like, trust, and respect. Without any of these qualities, you cannot succeed. Take the time to truly learn about your colleagues and you might be able to help in growing their business, resulting in a possible chance to grow your own.

SUDS

Network Online

Perhaps you feel overwhelmed already with all of your work, your "to do" lists, and your e-mail, but I urge you to devote your time, energy, and effort towards at least one online social networking site: LinkedIn, Facebook, or MySpace are options.

LinkedIn, created in 2003, has more than 9 million members. The average user is 39 and makes almost $140,000 per year. Its demographics are so desirable that while membership is free, advertising is expensive and lucrative for advertisers who account for about one-third of the revenue. But why should you join? Because your network allows you to tap into your friends' networks electronically. With a simple click of the mouse, you can connect with contacts who are up to three degrees away. This exponential arithmetic affords you the chance to "meet" online your most desirable prospects, contacts, leads, and colleagues. It also gives you the opportunity to reconnect with past colleagues with whom you've lost contact. In my case, it was a pleasant surprise to reconnect with Steve Edwards, who is now heading up Fresh Start Surgical Gifts. All of these connections therefore become a "warm" call rather than a cold call.

Both Facebook and MySpace are viewed as geared towards a younger crowd that has more time, effort, and sometimes, I think, computer acumen than me to create cool wallpaper, post mini-applications, share their favorite songs and photos. The fastest growing demographic, however, is adults over the age of 25. These two sites remain the behemoths in the industry with each averaging over 115 million visitors to their sites every month. In the US, however, Facebook remains number-one with 36 million American visitors. If networking is a numbers game to you, this is where you should be playing.

Specialized Online Social Networking Sites

If you feel particularly isolated or are looking to connect with industry-specific sites, a few have sprung up to fill the void. Sermo.com is only for US licensed physicians. In an unusual twist, you can easily remain anonymous, but your credentials must be real. The goal here is really doctors helping other doctors with diagnoses and the like. This demographic, in particular, is so overworked, time-stressed, and hard to reach that advertisers pay $100,000 to $150,000 per year just to have access to monitor discussions and ask feedback on new drugs and medical devices in development.

InMobile.org is just for the wireless industry, Reuters Space is for the financial industry, BlockSavvy.com is an urban, hip hop site, and AdGabber.com is for advertising and marketing professionals. Posting, commenting, and uploading videos, especially on AdGabber, will raise your profile, position you as the expert, and allow opportunities to knock at your door.

Your Online Reputation

As you post online, remember that your words, photos, and comments are often cached in the Web for years. Over one-third of all hiring managers respond that they will "Google" all applicants and 10 percent of all college admissions offers look at social networking sites to evaluate applicants. Of those colleges, a whopping 38 percent said that what they saw negatively impacted their view. So, as much as building your brand online is desirable, it can also hurt.

In recent years, we have witnessed a proliferation of negative sites created specifically for the purpose of "dissing" a big brand name. Starbucked.com, ihatestarbucks.com, and boycottwalmart.org, have all been snapped up by disgruntled customers and employees. The Wall Street Journal reports that Xerox has registered over twenty unflattering domains including xeroxstinks.com, xeroxcorporationsucks.com, and ihatezerox.com, obviously to prevent negative sites from sprouting. And, get this? Over 20,000 names are registered that end with "sucks.com."

Internet experts disagree as to whether or not you should buy out these offensive domains even as a preventive step. Southwestsucks, for example, redirects Web visitors to its official customer service complaint area, whereas Starbucks views its sites as just another indicator of how passionate people are about its brand.

Bank of America has the dubious distinction of having one of the most successful disgruntled sites. BankofAmericaSucks.com is one of the top fifteen results in a Google search for the banking giant, and thousands voice their opinion there daily. Bank of America admits to monitoring the postings, but doesn't appear to be taking resulting action.

For you, of course, the first step in managing your reputation is monitoring it. I have set up Google Alerts (www.googlealert.com) on my name, company name, and book title. Every day, whether in an article, blog, podcast, or posting, I receive a link to what's new. I even found out that one of the stories in which I had been quoted had been reprinted by the Wall Street Journal!

If, of course, the news flowing in is all positive, good for you! If it's negative, you have to determine if it's a legal libel, defamation, or trademark issue. Most of the time, it's not an easy or quick legal issue that can be resolved, but a freedom of speech issue. What you can do, however, is counterpunch with a positive news campaign. Terry Boothman, of Netsmartz, has the following suggested tactics:

- **Brand and Identity Management**—Saturate blogs, forums, journals, or news feeds with positive content to reverse any current damage.

- **Search Engine Optimization**—Post new content on your Web site in order to boost your rankings in the engines. The objective is to replace offensive listings with positive ones.

- **Social Media Optimization**—Leveraging such online magnets as MySpace, YouTube, or even eBay pages.

- **New Domains**—Buy, build, and create new sites offering positive content about your business.

MONEY SAVING TIP *In order to monitor your online brand, set up a quick, easy, and free alert at googlealert.com. You can pick the frequency of the alerts—once a day or once per week—and receive links to postings about you, your company, employer or competitor. How cool!*

YOUR TURN TO ACT

1. **Test Your Hook**—Every 7-second hook needs a reality test. At the next event, simply try your new hook and read the reaction. Is it working? Are folks giving you a confused look, or are they nodding their heads with understanding?

2. **Get There Early**—The secret to networking is lingering. You must get there early and stay late. Always put it on your calendar to arrive promptly without intrusive meetings beforehand and commitments after.

3. **Plan Your Networking Outfit**—Ensure that it reflects your brand and your style, that business cards in the outfit are easily accessible, and that your shoes are comfortable. Looking good but being in pain won't help you network.

4. **Order Your Name Badge Today**—Order two or three in case you lose one. Get a strong, easy-to-read badge that even includes your logo. And, if you are a woman who hates ruining her silk blouses by poking a hole through them, try a name badge that is held on with magnets. They work great!

5. **Network Online**—Determine if any of the social networking sites are right for you.

6. **Monitor Your Online Reputation**—Set up your Google Alerts today!

Chapter 13

Fueling Your Brand
Mastering Public Relations to Get the Word Out and the Revenue In

Pair the correct subject area with the famous expert:

SUBJECT AREA	EXPERT
1. Personal Finance	A Cesar Millan
2. Consumer Fraud	B Walter Mossberg
3. Your Health	C Dr. Oz
4. Home Decorating	D Jack Trout
5. Dog Training	E Jean Chatzky
6. Positioning	F David Horowitz
7. Technology	G Nate Berkus

In order to fully reap the benefits of your personal brand, you must create high awareness. An easy, free strategy is to use PR (public relations) as a branding vehicle.

WORDS of "*LIZ*DOM"

PUBLICITY BEGETS MORE PUBLICITY

Another unexpected bonus from being in the media is that publicity begets more publicity. In other words, when you are quoted one time as a source, other reporters on the same subject will also see the first story and then come back to you for quips and quotes.

Publicity Brings Visibility, Credibility, and Clients

Many PR professionals will caution you not to expect a direct return on your investment from publicity efforts. Instant credibility and higher visibility, they'll argue, are more attainable goals. I both agree and disagree; you'll reap the credibility and visibility, but you can also easily track leads. Most prospects will tell you that they just read about you, heard you on the news, or saw you on TV. And, if you want to track your leads a little better, make sure to ask every single caller how they heard about you, so you can get your arms around the marketing tools that are working best.

When I launched The Nuancing Group in 1997, the first thing I did was start talking to the media. In fact, I was on the front page of the San Diego Business Journal in a four-color photo before my business cards were even printed. Within two hours of the paper hitting subscribers, I was called by HNC Software about helping them create a new brand name. Bottom line? The contract was worth over $50,000!

Wendy Lieberman is a master of the media. If there is an article about retail trends, she'll be quoted. She speaks in good sound bites, and she only talks about her area of expertise. It's a sure-fire way for her to ring up sales for her company, WSL Strategic Retail.

Creating a Contest

Instead of waiting for the media to call you, you might try creating so much noise that the media is compelled to contact you. Creating contests is a great gimmick. These have traditionally worked well, but now work even harder , thanks to the power of viral marketing on the Web.

The Pillsbury Bake-Off has been crowning winners to much fanfare since 1949 and this year's winner also received a hot grand prize of $1 million. And, proving that the Dough Boy can enter the digital age, the contest also had an online component where Web visitors could vote for their favorite recipe.

The Duck brand of duct tape received over 2,500 entries for its "Saves the Day" contest, in which entrants had to tell the story of how this ubiquitous product was utilized in a "nick of time" situation to save the day. WD-40 perennially invites this type of feedback. The best WD-40 story? A woman who sprays the product on her front yard tree to prevent the squirrels from climbing up!

A contest not only provides publicity, but also gives you a database of new prospects and customers, generates goodwill, and promotes your brand and positioning.

You want to create a contest that brings in entries and curious con-

COMPANY SPECIALTY	CONTEST IDEA
Office Furniture	*"The messiest office"*
Construction/remodel Company	*"The home most in need of a makeover"*
Any food product	*"Recipe contest"*
Marketing/Graphic Design	*"The worst brochure ever!"*
Unusual Product	*"Weirdest use of your product"*
Miscellaneous Service	*"Create an ad for our company"*
Book Store	*"Best fiction, children's book or even simply best first chapter"*

sumers, but remains relevant to your brand.

Publicity Helps Your Web Presence

All of your attributions in the media also help your Google rankings. Since we assume that *The New York Times* has more readers than your Web site, just being quoted in such a large, respected outlet with a hot link to your site will exponentially raise your rankings. Remember: incoming links to your site, not outgoing links, are part of the Search Engine Optimization (SEO) formula.

Get Listed as an Expert

To start the ball rolling as an expert, I recommend that you list yourself with a host of Web sites and services. Below is just a beginning list. In preparing your online bio and area of expertise, pay close attention to your brand: clearly define your niche for reporters. Let them know the types of stories and specific expertise that you can provide. Note that most of these sites have an average cost of about $250 per year. Do I think it's worth this investment? You betcha!

http://www.sources.com/QuickListing-SAL454.pdf (about $350/year)

http://www.web-directories.ws/

http://www.powerreporting.com/category/People_finders/Experts/

http://www.allexperts.com/central/expert.htm (free!)

http://www.experts.com/ ($250/year)

http://www.guestfinder.com/ ($250/yr)

Responding to Reporters' Queries

To get into the news, you can not only list yourself as an expert and wait for reporters to contact you, but you can also reverse the game and respond to queries from reporters. Really! Reporters need experts on the Gulf War, developers who worked on the I-Phone, fashion forecasters, mortgage brokers, and just about every expert you can think of. Top sites are:

http://www.helpareporter.com/ (free!)

http://www.reporterconnection.com/ (free!)

https://profnet.prnewswire.com/

http://www.prleads.com/

By responding to a query a few years ago, I became the branding columnist for *Entrepreneur* magazine. And, to get even more personal branding examples for this book, I also posted a query. Now, having seen the hundreds of e-mails that poured in, I can give you a few tips to ensure that your response hits the mark.

1. **Be Succinct**—Yes, I'm interested in your answer, but not pages and pages of it.

2. **Give Me a Taste**—Great responses list one to three solid ideas and then offer to talk in more detail if interested.

3. **Do Not Simply Send Them to Your Site**—I received hundreds of responses that told me I can see their branding at www.whatever.com. I even received one that simply said, "Google me!" I repeat: a reporter will not go to your site to find an answer; you must give one.

4. **Avoid Ruthless Self-Promotion**—I clearly understand that you want to be in the news, but remember: you are not the story. Responses should be neutral, fact-based, and with ideas and suggestions for readers or listeners.

5. **Provide Full Contact Info**—Countless times I received e-mails with a name only, no company name, Web site, or phone number. You can't get publicity without a reporter getting in touch with you!

Media Rules

One of the best ways to get in the media is to be quoted as an expert. During any interview, here are a few rules to follow:

- **Must Be Your Area of Expertise**—If the reporter's query is only tangentially relevant to your topic area, stay away. You only want to become branded in your niche. I thought I had hit the jackpot a few years ago when a reporter from *The New York Times* left a message on my voice mail about wanting to interview me. His story for which he wanted quotes? How Israel can brand itself in the wake of the instability in the Middle East. It broke my heart, but I didn't comment. I am an expert on branding individuals, companies, and products; I know nothing about politics!

- **Immediately Respond to Queries**—Since most reporters are under stringent deadlines, the first one to return the phone call usually gets into the story.

- **Accuracy Is #1**—If you don't know the answer, say you don't, but under no circumstances should you invent a statistic or research fact.

- **Always Ask the Deadline**—Sometimes, a reporter is working on a longer lead-time as in a front page magazine article. Knowing the deadline means you can prepare your comments and even schedule a "meaty" phone call at a later date and time.

- **Do as Many Interviews in Person as Possible**—Although the beauty of the phone means that you can remotely call-in for your radio interview, don't! If you can drive to the station, seize the opportunity. It's a way to build rapport and even a long-term relationship with the host. Further, if you are new to radio, sitting in the studio and talking directly to the hosts with eye contact usually produces better insightful discussion and results.

- **If Calling In, Stand Up**—By standing up for your phone interview, you immediately lift your diaphragm, resulting in better voice quality. As we noted in Chapter 6 on voice, the tonal quality of your voice influences perception.

- **Eliminate Distractions**—Before an interview, turn off your cell phone, turn your computer either off or on mute, close your office door, silence your children, and focus. Do you think I'm kidding? I've heard cell phones ring, dogs bark, and kids interrupt on business interviews. Don't let it happen to you!

- **Have Pre-Determined Sound Bites**—Before you call a reporter, before you answer one question or appear on TV, make sure you know the top three points you want to make. They can be announcing your new book, positioning you as the expert, providing two tips for teens in stress, the secret to saving money in this economy, etc. But, you must be prepared. With an average appearance on TV coming in at just over two minutes, you must be succinct.

- **Practice Aloud**—Practicing aloud makes you notice how your quote will sound. It will tell you whether it is too long or complicated.

- **Look at the Interviewer**—You are having a conversation with the reporter, not the camera. Engaging with the interviewer makes for better TV. Chris Saunders, former news anchor for KFMB, knows that eye contact can make or break an interview. Remain engaged.

- **Use a Land Line**—Nothing annoys a radio producer more than poor sound quality, dropped calls, and cell phone static. Get a land line and immediately disable call waiting!

- **Stay Relaxed**—Viewers and listeners can feel your anxiety or comfort level. I've seen waiting guests listen to their I-Pods, take deep breaths, or even stretch back stage to ensure that they can project an aura of cool and calm.

MARK DIMASSIMO

As co-founder of Tappening.com, which promotes drinking tap water, Mark DiMassimo has mastered sound bites. Listen to this one: "...being charged for water is like being charged for gravity." It's a great way of positioning the fact that bottled drinking water is getting all washed up!

- **Never Insult the Host/The Host Is Always Right**—These are the golden rules of media. No matter what, they are the host and you are the guest. They have a contract and you don't. When I was introduced on radio in Texas as the author of "*Done Marketing*" (vs. *DUH! Marketing*), I didn't immediately pipe up and correct them. Instead, I quickly quipped, "you're right, boys, I done wrote that book called DUH! Marketing."

I recently saw a disastrous TV interview with my fun and former neighbor, Sam Zien, the Cooking Guy. On *The Today Show*, he had the chutzpah to tell Kathie Lee Gifford to be quiet: "there's a lot of chatter here, can I just talk?" His comments caused quite a whirlwind Web stir, with most folks blogging that he's become the poster child of rude. He did get invited back, but they brought him back with an etiquette expert who chastised him for not being respectful and charming. Of course, all of this publicity boosted his profile, but in my world, I'd rather be the gracious guest.

WORDS of "LIZDOM"

THE GOLDEN RULE OF MEDIA

Always remember that the host is always right. You are the gracious guest who is charming and reacts to his lead. Although you have your talking points, you must follow the lead of the host at all times.

SUDS

And, here's one special tip: if you would like a copy of your TV, radio, or Web interview, please make sure to inquire about it in advance so that they can record it for you. Often, after the segment has aired, it is too late. Also, the current operating procedure is for you to bring your own blank media such as a DVD +R or CD-R. Don't forget to put your name and mailing address on the jewel case and on the disc.

Media Training

Before most CEOs step in front of the camera, a publicist ensures that they have spent at least eight hours in media training. Topics covered include looking at the right camera, gesturing correctly, sitting up straight (really!), practicing your key talking points, answering questions, deflecting blame, and the like.

If you opt not to invest in media training, then here's a little secret: start your media small. Or, let's put it this way: practice makes perfect. I'm thrilled that my early interviews were in small, local papers. In the Richmond Business Journal, for instance, I made the monumental mistake of using a big word before stopping and spelling it for the reporter. As a result, I look like a fool with this quote: "a good way to increase recall of names is a literazation." I actually said, "alliteration." Ooops! I've never made that mistake again!

DR. LISA B (BOESKY)

Dr. Lisa Boesky is the author of *When to Worry: How to Tell If Your Teen Needs Help—And What to Do About It.* She understands what she is and what she isn't. She turned down an appearance on Oprah because it was outside of her core competency: talking about teens in crisis. She has maximized her visibility, however, by hammering this topic home with appearances on *The Early Show, The O'Reilly Factor,* and *CNN.* Good show!

Another path on the way to continuous improvement is keeping an archive of every article, radio, or TV interview. Review it closely and note at least three areas for improvement. If possible, try to enlist your Council Members to make helpful suggestions. With enough practice, you'll eventually be ready for your close-up on Oprah!

Writing By-Lined Articles to Build Your Reputation

If you're not fond of being in front of the camera or being grilled by reporters, you might find writing articles, opinion pieces, or letters to the editor a more favorable route. Peter MacCracken, of Strategic Communications, hopes never to be on-camera, but his presence is felt through the power of his pen.

Business publications, women's magazines, and virtually all specialized media use freelancers and are at some point looking for content. You can first write a "query letter" to the editor; essentially, it is a pitch for your story, what it will cover, and most importantly, why it's timely and relevant to their readership.

You can also write articles just for the Web. So many newsletters are craving content! There are also article distribution services—a place where you submit the article once and then they circulate it for you. Check out:

www.submityourarticle.com
www.ezinearticles.com
www.articlemarketer.com
Ezine Articles- www.ezinearticles.com
Go Articles- www.goarticles.com
Buzzle- www.buzzle.com
Searchwarp- www.searchwarp.com
Article Base- www.articlebase.com
Article Dashboard- www.articleboard.com
Amazines- www.amazines.com
Article City- www.articlecity.com
Article Alley- www.articlealley.com
Idea Marketers- www.ideamarketers.com

How Articles Help You

In this era, the Web continues to dominate. Every article of yours is written because of the most powerful part of the story: the little section about you! This "about the author" section must quickly state your credentials and then give the readers a reason to come back to your site for even more. "For a free list of what never to do in media, please go to...."

Listing your articles at your own site also is valuable to visitors, and it increases your reach. Please ensure that your writing agreement allows you to retain the copyright, so that you can also reprint your own articles at your own site. Often, publications have as standard legalese that they own the copyright and any and all reproduction is prohibited.

If you are quoted as the expert or there is a major profile on you or your company, getting reprints is a huge promotional opportunity. Distribute them to prospects, clients, and colleagues. They are an instant credibility booster and should earn a place in your bio (ex: featured in *Business Week*) or your overview folder. Note: please reproduce legally; rights are typically very affordable.

YOUR TURN TO ACT

Prepare a Bio—Having this key document prepared and ready will help get you booked easily. It's a given that producers will request this 1-2 page biography.

Have a TV Outfit Ready To Go—Usually cameras disapprove of white, red, or loud patterns.

Create Story Ideas—In your press materials and on your Web site, list the instances when you should be called. Example: contact George Whalin for stories about retailing, retailing trends, and consumer shopping behavior.

Prepare Likely Interview Questions—Dr. Lisa Boesky has a great 2-pager at the ready and at her Web site for hosts. Remember: no host or producer will read your book in advance of your appearance.

Chapter 14

Taglines
How to Turn Up the Temperature

Pair the correct brand with its famous tagline:

TAGLINE	BRAND NAME
1. Got Milk?	A LV Convention & Visitors Bureau
2. Tastes Great—Less Filling	B California Milk Processor Board
3. In space, no one can hear you scream	C Papa John's
4. The Fabric of Our Lives	D Miller Lite
5. A Diamond is Forever	E The movie *Alien*
6. Better Ingredients, Better Pizza	F DeBeers
7. What Happens in Vegas Stays in Vegas	G Disneyland
8. The happiest place on earth	H Cotton

What Is a Tagline?

Taglines are the invisible communication today. They're rarely discussed, barely analyzed, and sparingly researched. Yet, a good tagline can provide the essential underpinning upon which to build all your marketing messages.

A tagline is a phrase that follows your brand name to explain your unique selling proposition. It differentiates you from your competitors, expresses your personality, and adds consistency to your marketing campaign. It should be such a natural outgrowth of your brand positioning that the two are inextricably linked. Remember "N-E-S-T-L-E-S: Nestle makes the very best chocolate?" Or "Memorex: Is it Live or is it Memorex?" Both of these are memorable taglines that differentiate the brands from their competitors.

I applauded Ernst & Young's move with its tagline. It took a common misperception among the business community and turned it into a positive. "From start to finish" acknowledges that although its competitors may not accomplish anything, Ernst &Young works with you from beginning to end. Just great!

WORDS of "*LIZ*DOM"

NO QUESTIONS ASKED

Questions rarely work as taglines; instead, focus on creating an "ownable" statement by using a unique or rarely used word in your industry.

SUDS

Avoiding Generic Flu

If you're not careful in creating an ownable tagline, your line may quickly deteriorate into a cliché. In the banking world, "bank on us" is applicable to any bank, but appropriate for none because it doesn't communicate a sound benefit. On the other hand, Citibank's pre-merger "The Citi never sleeps" line worked well because it communicated a 24-hour, accessible, reachable institution.

The "we mean business" line is also over-employed. Examples of businesses that have used this line abound from American Airlines to the City of Seattle. Again, the message is too generic to work well for any type of business, so keep it away from yours.

In the high tech and software world, everything seems to be a "robust, seamless, 24/7 solution." IBM actually coined the phrase "e-business solution," but never service marked it, leaving it to be copied by thousands of other companies.

Using Humor

Taglines are an excellent way to demonstrate your brand personality. Every time I read the huge billboards plastered with Camera World's tagline of "For negative people, I smile." The same holds true when I see Huggies' tagline: "We're behind you every step of the way." Or, how about SuperSoil? "If it's not SuperSoil, it's just plain old dirt."

WORDS of "*LIZ*DOM"

BIG BRANDS SPECIAL EXEMPTION

Famous brands can afford to use big, lofty taglines such as McDonald's "Lovin' it" or Allstate's "you're in good hands with Allstate." Smaller companies, however, must use very descriptive taglines that explain their narrowly defined market, such as Timken: "leader in bearings and steel" to PK Ware, "the data compression experts."

Rhyme Time

As I mentioned in the Chapter 3, rhymes are phenomenal mnemonic devices. Ask a colleague over the age of 30 to see if he or she can complete this phrase: "Takes a licking and..." Virtually all of them will complete

Timex's famous line with "keeps on ticking." Or, ask an even older friend or family member about this one: "You'll wonder where the yellow went when you brush your teeth with Pepsodent." In 1971, we added to our national vocabulary, "the quicker picker upper" from Bounty. Lysol will "disinfect to protect" and currently Ziploc is "designed with you in mind." See if a rhyme might work for your business.

Overcoming a Negative Brand Name

If it's impossible to change your brand name, a tagline can certainly help explain your business positioning. Schlotzky's Deli uses "Funny name, serious sandwich." El Pollo Loco's tagline basically translates its brand for the non-Spanish speaker with "When you're crazy for chicken." ING almost had no choice but to introduce its tagline of "It's not an ending, but a beginning" because of all of the confusion with its name.

Using Puns

Using a play on words can also raise recall. Skoal's tagline of "Always there in a pinch" certainly plays upon its smokeless tobacco. Or, Shiner Bock's "Brewed with attitude." I also like the Chicago-based restaurant called Rosebud: "A very rare steakhouse well done." Don't forget Lunchables: "We make fun of lunch."

Descriptive Tagline

Often, a good tagline is quite simple, such as Tyson's "We're chicken," or Quiznos' "Toasted Tastes Better." Or even Coleman: "The Outdoor Company"—it reinforces their narrow niche.

Owning Your Tagline

In a carefully crafted tagline, the key point of difference is either overtly stated or strongly implied. This strategy reinforces your positioning and preempts your competitor from using the same idea. Remember, the goal is to own a unique benefit in the customer's mind.

I remember receiving a business card from a coach with this tagline: "Helping companies go from good to great." My immediate question was "do you work with Jim Collins, author of the best-selling *Good to Great?*" Her answer was no, but she thought it was a good concept. Wrong! It's not only infringement on his book, but it also erroneously implies that she is a licensed consultant for his work, similar to Michael Gerber's successful franchising of The E-Myth.

MELISSA ADAMS

Melissa Adams, a copywriter, has a great tagline; it's both descriptive and a pun: "WordWorks: Your Write Hand." Write on!

Altoids has a phenomenal tagline: "The curiously strong mint." The word "curiously" is ownable, and if any other company tried to use the word, it would seem to invade the mindshare of this famous tin-packed mint. The same principle holds true with BMW's famous line, "The ultimate driving machine." If any other car company tried to use the word "machine," it would appear to have been manufactured by BMW.

When Coke introduced its new brand of Dasani water, its tagline was really a reassuring message to retailers: "Brought to you by Coca-Cola." The knowledge that it was a Coke product reassured retailers that its distribution system was already in place, unlike the service problems that plagued Red Bull and other new age beverages.

A good tagline should be so clear that even if your audience had never heard of your company, they could determine what business you're in.

WORDS of "*LIZ*DOM"

TEST IT ALOUD

Don't forget to explore how your tagline will sound when said aloud. If it's cumbersome or too long, it will probably be easily forgotten.

SUDS

Differentiating in a Crowded Market

When a market becomes overcrowded or a company name becomes confusingly similar, it is a good time to introduce a tagline. This statement is particularly applicable to the high-tech field in which the number of new companies appearing with the name "cyber" "micro" or "net" grows every day.

MYSTERIOUS GALAXY

Terry Gilman, and her partners Maryelizabeth Hart and Jeff Mariotte, actually created their alliterative tagline before their business had even been named! Sixteen years ago, they came together to create a bookstore stocking mystery, science fiction, and fantasy books. They didn't want to stock true crime and didn't want to bother with blood and other gory details. So, in the process of creating their name they came upon this beautiful tagline: "Books of Martians, Murder, Magic, and Mayhem." Their San Diego-based business continues to serve the community and its niche.

Use Consistency

When the US Army introduced "An army of one," every single person in the military recognized that this was a whopper of a burnout! Why? Because it goes against the key principle of the military: teamwork. This tagline makes me question whether or not I can now rely upon my fellow soldier because he is thinking just of himself and the ads are reinforcing this message!

A tagline should also serve as an acid test: if your brochure, advertising campaign, or sales letter conflict with the tagline, it's obviously time to rethink your creative message.

Don't Change before It's Time

You will grow tired of your tagline way before your customers ever will. Resist the urge to change! Taglines are part of your positioning, your legacy, and therefore should change infrequently. Look at these time-tested taglines:

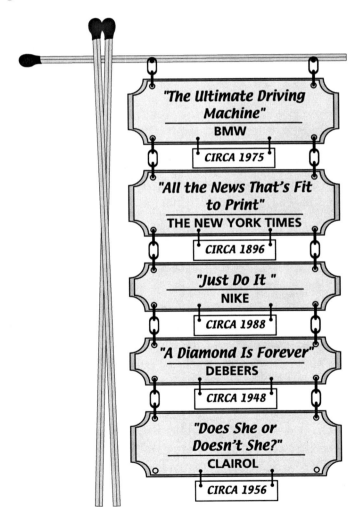

"The Ultimate Driving Machine"
BMW
CIRCA 1975

"All the News That's Fit to Print"
THE NEW YORK TIMES
CIRCA 1896

"Just Do It "
NIKE
CIRCA 1988

"A Diamond Is Forever"
DEBEERS
CIRCA 1948

"Does She or Doesn't She?"
CLAIROL
CIRCA 1956

General Electric (GE) had one of the most memorable taglines in recent history: "We bring good things to life." It is estimated that over 80 percent of consumers could recall their tagline. Wow! A few years ago, however, the company wanted to make sure customers understood that it stands for more than just light bulbs, so it introduced "Imagination at Work." Now that's original. Advertisers would kill for the sort of mindshare that GE had, but GE has decided to throw it all away for a generic, vanilla tagline. "Imagination at Work" is a phrase that is used for hundreds of products, from a line of elementary reading books to a course you can purchase for $99. This idea is just another example of how the lights are on, but nobody's home.

Hellman's mayonnaise kept its tagline for thirty-seven years before changing it in May 2002 from "Bring out the Hellmann's; Bring out the best" to "Hellman's at its best." Ford Motor Co. changed its tagline to "Built Ford tough," after having used "Have you driven a Ford lately?" for over fifteen years. In 2007, Gerber dropped "Shouldn't your baby be a Gerber baby?" and instead adopted, "Anything for baby."

The two behemoths in advertising today who frequently and mistakenly change their tagline are McDonald's and Coca-Cola. In 1886, Coke started with "Drink Coca-Cola," introduced "It's the Real Thing" in 1969, used "Coke is in" in 1982, and in 1986 brought us "The Coke Side of Life." McDonald's started with "Look for the Golden Arches" in 1960, then introduced "You Deserve a Break Today" in 1971, and the famous "Two all-beef patties, special sauce, lettuce, cheese, pickle, onions, on a sesame seed bun" in 1975—a tagline that only lasted one year! I'll bet that we baby boomers can recite that recipe in our dreams. Today, I hope that you're "Lovin' it."

If the goal is to create a tagline that will last for the foreseeable future, you're best served by avoiding "of the moment" taglines. I had a good chuckle when no fewer than three companies, including AT&T started using "Ka-ching!" That line now sounds so very 1999. Or, how about the state of Washington, which came out with "Say WA," as in "say

Washington." Clearly, you can hear the homage to "Whazz up?" The city of Seattle committed an even bigger sin by introducing "Metronatural" as its tagline. In 2006, the buzz was all about metrosexual men, but now that moment has come and thankfully left.

Tagline Guidelines

How do you carefully craft and employ a tagline? Although there's no secret formula in this highly subjective area, here are a few guidelines:

- **Ensure that it is consistent with the brand name and positioning—** make sure that the brand and its phrase aren't in conflict.

- **Convey the message in consumer language—**forget about using industry jargon and speak in plain English.

- **Communicate one simple idea—**trying to convey two ideas doubles your chance that neither message will be remembered.

- **Opt for a few, short words—**in our society, we want short, quick messages.

- **Always use the tagline on the product, in advertising, and in all communication—**this includes your business cards, proposals, letterhead, etc.

- **Test the tagline—**if it's a little bit risqué, don't be afraid to ask your customers or consumers for their reaction.

- **Create a tagline that is "ownable" and cannot be usurped by your competitors—**look for unusual words or phrases.

- **Avoid all acronyms or initials—**letters quickly dissolve into alphabet soup without any recalled message.

- **Keep in the present tense—**If you remember your English grammar, use the present progressive (i.e., "ing") as in "working towards a better future."

- **Ensure that it is linguistically sound—**no tongue twisters allowed.

1. **Test Your Tagline**—Before committing to a tagline, narrow the choices and pick from three to five favorites. Convene your Council and test reactions. Then, include it onto a few electronic documents or e-mails. Call the recipients and check reaction again.

2. **Google Your Tagline**—Make sure no one else is using your tagline already.

Chapter 15

Brand Building
How to Keep the Flame Alive and Avoid Burnout

Pair the famous icon with the familiar brand:

ICON	BRAND NAME
1. Umbrella	A Burberry's
2. Swoosh	B Nike
3. Red Chile	C Citibank (formerly Traveler's Insurance)
4. Golden Arches	D Chili's
5. Brown Shopping Bag	E Michael Jordan
6. Beige, Red, Camel Plaid	F Bloomingdale's
7. Mickey Mouse Ears	G McDonald's
8. #23	H Disney

The Magic Three in Top of Mind Awareness

Top of mind awareness is the secret to staying at the top of the decision tree; people must think of you in order to do business with you. Marketers will often refer to the "magic of three." This magic formula simply means that most consumers can easily rattle off three competitors in a category: phone company, rental company, consulting company, etc. After three, the going gets tough and prospects truly start digging deep to come up with competitors. Your goal, therefore, is to always shoot to the top of your prospects' minds.

WORDS of "*LIZ*DOM"

GETTING INTO "THE MAGIC THREE"

Your goal is to secure a place in your prospect's mind so that you are one of the top three brands that they think of in your category. Reinforce your brand name whenever possible.

Keeping Your Name in front of Prospects

One easy way to literally keep your name in front of prospects is to place it when and where they are. Bill Howe Plumbing always puts stickers on customers' pipes just in case there is a leak. Discount Purifiers of San Diego places its information on water filters, and 1-800-APPLIANCE supplies magnets for your refrigerator to increase recall.

Sean Farrell, a top Mercedes Benz salesmen, succeeds by being a wealth of information about the great bells and whistles found on the new models. One of my favorite tactics is that he programs his phone number into your car's phone memory database. He's always there when you need him. Vrroom!

I often hear erroneously that you should be competing for "share of desk" if your decision making occurs within a traditional office setting. No! You are still competing for share of mind. In today's world, the printed Post-It notes, cheap pens, mouse pads, and free notepads with your logo no longer bring results. And, if you are going up against the Big Boys who have deeper pockets, you must earn top of mind awareness through strategic brand planning and innovative premiums.

Premiums That Relate to Your Brand Promise and Positioning

I'm asking you to correlate all of your premiums, sometimes called "trash and tschochkes" to your brand promise and positioning. So, if you are an orthodontist, like Dr. Melanie Parker, your pen isn't an ordinary pen, but a severely crooked one that represents the state of her patients' teeth. Or, perhaps it is a simple fly swatter, compliments of Lloyd's Pest Control. Or, Cajun spice seasoning given to me in New Orleans by conference sponsor Don Lintzen of Ciara Group with the tag of "Add a Dash of Spice to Your Marketing." Or, breath mints given by the conveniently named law firm of Mintz, Levin, Cohn, Ferris, Glovsky and Pepeo. Or, a simple pack of tissues brought to you by the makers of Tamiflu. And, my favorite, a 3? inch pen that doubles in size upon a push of a button and proudly displays the brand name Levitra!

MONEY SAVING TIP *A welcome and inexpensive premium is a bookmark. You can design and even print it yourself. Laminate it and you have a tool that increases its longevity.*

How to Use Your Premiums

Your premium puts you in the bonus round. You can send one with every single thank-you card; it can be your key follow-up piece. You, of course, can distribute it at trade shows, but if you're like me, a small business, I think it is perfect at Chamber meetings or other networking events where you have the chance to set-up a small display table.

Also remember that you might want to have different premiums for different levels of commitment. It's OK not to treat every client the same. You might, for example, have bigger holiday presents for your clients who spend the most money with you. By the same token, after you finish an assignment, you might want to give a "thanks for the business" token that varies upon the size of the account. I do this type of sorting with my business as well: the top clients receive a Tiffany magnifying glass (The Nuancing Group's logo) from Paloma Picasso, whereas smaller clients receive a simple glass one.

BOBBIN BEAM

Voice-over artist Bobbin Beam knows that prospects must hear her before they can hire her. Her ingenious idea? She's taken a box of Whitman's iconic chocolate sampler and turned it the Bobbin's Voice-Over Sampler. Delicious idea!

RED HOT
EXAMPLE

Your Car as a Roving Billboard

Today, your car remains a free and mobile billboard. It can be as simple as creating a bumper sticker. The Women's Institute for Financial Education has a bumper sticker that is unforgettable: "A Man is Not a Plan." Note that even if they turn their brand name into an acronym against my advice, it humorously spells WIFE!

Your license frame can work hard for you. Racetrack fans proudly drive around Del Mar with "Where the turf meets the surf." Or, you can sell or give away frames that promote your brand. I've seen cow-printed, Swarovski-studded, heart-printed, skull-etched and palm tree-flowing designs that portray a certain feeling.

Just because you're serving business professionals, don't think you have to be conservative and boring.

PENNY PRITZKER

When Penny Pritzker, 42, launched the Parking Spot in 1998, the off-airport parking market was highly fragmented and no competitor claimed a strong-hold. The firm's goal was to consolidate the industry and woo frequent business travelers with consistent and reliable service.

The original logo, plastered on the company's shuttle buses, reflected a ho-hum image—a silver background with a "P" centered on a yield sign. The issue? The Parking Spot's buses looked just like the buses of their myriad parking competitors. The Parking Spot was ready to go bold. After all, "the biggest idea is usually the scariest," proclaims Mark Wildman, the company's vice president of marketing. In 2000, the Parking Spot unveiled a new design: black spots of different sizes dancing against a vibrant yellow background.

The results have been astounding: Revenues at facilities that have been open at least one year are up 40 percent. And customers couldn't forget the dotted shuttle they rode in on. Although the redesign was a drastic change, it didn't detour from the brand's customer service roots. The secret was to demonstrate that the company could be tongue-in-cheek, yet still take seriously the job of transporting customers to the airport. Slogans plastered across the buses blare, "Think this looks ridiculous? Try missing your flight." Or, "If you have a spotty memory, this oughta help." Extra service touches such as bottled water upon disembarking, complimentary copies of USA Today, free car battery jumps, and direct car-to-terminal service deliver on the brand promise. Sometimes bold and brash really does hit the spot.

In 2005, when Marla Levitt started her Pawz Pet Taxi in Chicago, one of her first purchases was a Chrysler Town and Country Minivan. She immediately had it painted as her company mascot, so that it looked like a big yellow taxi with paw prints. All around the expressway, her car barked its message to drivers, leading to both business and heightened brand awareness.

Western Bank of Clovis also used cars as its advertising "vehicle" and had two Volkswagens designed as actual piggy banks on wheels, complete with snouts and coin slots. And, don't forget how The Geek Squad pulls up in its signature Volkswagens with stark black and white coloring.

I also adore vanity license plates and use one myself. But, here's a quick warning: don't ever try to have a clandestine relationship with one of these bulls' eyes on your car. I get e-mails and honks all the time from people seeing me on the road!

Real estate agents pretty much led the way towards using magnetic signs on their vehicles to promote their businesses, but it works for other occupations as well. The latest ones are affordable, have a quick turnaround, and can easily be taken off when you want to get out of "on mode." Sean Wolff, of Attention To Detail, uses magnetized signs on his flaming red truck. He not only promotes his brand, but he also lives it as well with his immaculately clean vehicle.

Valentine Viannay's business is named The Painted Genie, and not surprisingly, her car is painted with her logo, name, phone number and Web site. Kidz-n-Fun has a trailer with high energy graphics of kids tumbling, jumping, and perfectly representing its gymnastic business.

Power of Snail Mail

Since it seems as if everyone has switched all of their communication to e-mail, you might be able to break through the clutter and secure more top of mind awareness through the good ol' fashioned post office. Pam Russell of Send Out Cards recognizes the bonds that can be strengthened with a quick follow-up. She sends thank-you cards, holiday cards, nice-to-meet-you cards, congratulations cards, and often adds in a little gift. If you want to forgo a computer-interfaced system, Vanessa Rogers of Hand Did by Viv creates branded, hand-made cards just for your business. And Julie Dunsmore offers handmade scented cards at logorama.com. These expressions will never be forgotten.

An Extra Thank You

If you want to grow your business and get word-of-mouth referrals, never forget the "thank you," especially when it is unexpected. Virtually all of us feel under-appreciated, and I have yet to meet someone who feels over-thanked. I remember the brouhaha with NFL player Terrell Owens (TO) who was feeling under-appreciated even though he was making over $22 million a year.

A thank-you can take many forms: a phone call, an e-mail, or a card as discussed above. But, my favorite is the thank-you with a little treat. I hand-write thank-you cards and include a $10 gift card to Starbucks, Blockbuster, or Barnes & Noble. Follow-up communication can work, but it must be immediate and appropriate. Although your Hallmark card might suffice, be leery of overtly emotional, sentimental cards; they just don't work well for business.

Actress Carol Louise is always remembered for her uncommon thank you. She rewards hotel and service personnel with $2 bills, and at Halloween, luscious candy as well. As a result, return visits are greeted with warm enthusiasm and extra special service. This is a hot tip, indeed!

WORDS of "*LIZ*DOM"

IMMEDIATE FOLLOW-UP

In order to harness the power of a thank-you or a referral, stock your drawer immediately with cards, stamps, and gift cards. If you have to take a special trip out to buy Barnes & Noble gift cards, for example, your wishes will be delayed.

SUDS

Thinking of Your Prospects

We may often think of our prospects, but we must let them know when we do. A great example is often exhibited by specialty retailers. They call when special merchandise might be perfect for you! Leann Wynder of Sweetpea Children's Clothing store calls her clients upon new shipment arrivals. Nordstrom superstars also use a good database to make friendly reminders not only about appropriate merchandise, but also about upcoming birthday and anniversary gifts as well.

Seeing a relevant article for your clients and sending them a copy is also a good way to stay in front of your customers. You can send these items either electronically or through snail mail.

YOUR TURN TO ACT

Immediately plan your thank-you course of action. Stock your office with cards, stamps, gift cards, or an online service (such as Send Out Cards) to minimize the time between the good deed and the thank-you.

Create an action plan for your car to work as your billboard. Explore magnetic signs (buildasign.com, bigdaddysigns.com, etc.), vanity license plates, bumper stickers, and even a car wrap.

Think strategically about creating a brand-appropriate premium. Start the design, procurement, and estimating process today!

Chapter 16

Fan the Flames
Branding Big on a Small Budget

Pair the famous Super Bowl celebrity
with the familiar brand:

SUPER BOWL CELEBRITY	BRAND NAME
1. Bouncing Brunette, Candice Michelle	A NFL
2. P. Diddy, Justin Timberlake	B Diamond Emerald Nuts
3. Kevin Federline	C Go Daddy
4. Leonard Nimoy	D Pepsi
5. Martha Stewart, David Beckham	E Aleve
6. Robert Goulet	F Bud Light
7. Carlos Mencia	G Nationwide Insurance

If you're like most small and service businesses, I gather that you don't want to spend $100,000 per second to advertise in the 2010 Super Bowl. Instead, let's look at ways that are more efficient.

Sponsoring an Event

I am a huge proponent of this type of marketing; it gets your name out to your target market and often for the big, fat price of free! Every year San Diego sponsors the Rock n' Roll Marathon, for example. Of course, we expect sponsors such as Foot Locker and New Balance, but local sponsors such as Spa Velia can also donate their services. Can we say "massage, please?" There are even opportunities for the goodie bags, which are a great way to distribute your premium (see Chapter 15), coupons, or special promotions.

In-kind services are usually welcome, especially if you can donate printing, graphic design, computer services (registration information, contact management, etc.), e-mail marketing services, marketing services (creating the theme and copy), legal services (reviewing contracts), and the like.

Every single event looking for sponsors typically prepares a one-sheet fact page detailing number of impressions, demographic information, expected media coverage, etc. If this information does not match your intended target, do not sign on. Again, your goal remains to market efficiently to the right target at the right time.

Founder Carolyn Crowley of Myriad Software sponsored the eighth race at the Del Mar Thoroughbred Club. The race was named after her company, and she had the privilege of presenting the trophy in the winner's circle. Total cost? Less than $5,000.

You can also create your own event, even on a small-scale. Chef Paul Canales of restaurant Oliveto created an annual Tomato Dinner in 1990 that consistently sells out weeks ahead. Everything on the menu from appetizer to dessert is based upon locally grown tomatoes. In 2001, Barona Casino started its annual RibFest that has gamblers anxiously awaiting the event.

Working with Charities

I'm always amazed at how quickly folks forget that there is a way of doing well by doing good. After the horrific fires that plagued Southern California in October of 2007, numerous companies stepped up to the plate in brand-appropriate ways. PETCO rescued and housed hundreds of animals; Qualcomm donated its stadium and made in-kind donations. The law firm of Morrison & Foerster published an amazing handbook simply entitled *Helping Handbook for Individuals and Small Businesses Affected by the 2007 Southern California Wildfires*. It explains the legal issues that most of us (certainly me) don't understand under these circumstances.

3 HOT SHOES

Joanna Herr Hanks, Brandy Sebastian, and Jake Hesseltine formed 3 Hot Shoes in 2008 to photograph marathons, mud runs, and the like. The intriguing photo finish? They give a portion of the revenues received from every event back to the organizing charity. Hot indeed!

But, it's not just disasters that should trigger effort. Donating to a live or silent auction returns more than just goodwill; it builds brand awareness via the charity's publicity efforts, catalogs, and live events. It generates trials, especially if you have given a certificate where the customer must still come to your office or store for redemption, and may ultimately cement customer loyalty if trial leads to brand loyalty.

Liberty Tax Service tied in to the Blood Bank and gave away free tax audits to donors. Chipotle tied in with National Library Sign-Up Month to give away a free lunch or dinner just by showing your library card.

Speak Your Way out of Obscurity

There are two options for public speaking: 1) self-hosted or 2) organization-, association-, or company-hosted. The easiest method, at least early on in your career, is clearly the second option where someone invites you to speak. The company or group handles all of the logistics, room procurement, meal service, registration, name badges, etc. Your job is to show up and present compelling information.

Speaking in this manner in your area of expertise pays enormous dividends whether you get paid or not. The sponsoring organization typically blasts their meeting announcement with your credentials via e-mail a few times, resulting in free advertising. Further, if you are perceived as the expert, then you have the opportunity to select the right speaking gigs so that you are presenting to your ideal target customer!

If you are presenting within your company to other colleagues, other departments, or in other countries, it raises your profile and solidifies you as the expert on that topic.

Audience members often run up to the speaker and cannot wait to do business with them. They think to themselves, "if this amount of knowledge is what the speaker can give away, can you imagine what he or she could do for me if I actually paid?"

Of course, you would do yourself and your audience a tremendous disservice if your talk was completely promotional. Instead, it should be a true, fact-based program that informs and arms your listener with practical ideas, tactics, and suggestions.

You can easily find these organizations through e-mail notices, association bulletins, and through Internet research. Regardless of your specialty, there is an association out there that would be delighted to have you share your wisdom. Remember to assemble all of your material on publicity from Chapter 13: your bio and picture, plus an overview including at least three things audience members will learn.

At every speech, offer a raffle prize drawn from the business cards put in your designated bowl. This technique allows you to build your all-important database that you'll need for follow-up. Never rely upon the hosting organization to provide you with a list of attendees; it won't happen, despite good intentions.

Another secret is to distribute evaluation forms to your audience. If you are new as a speaker, it allows you the much-needed feedback. Of course, it also allows you to ask for a testimonial or ask if they would like you to contact them about consulting.

Teach a Class

A variation of this speaking theme is teaching a class. I've guest lectured many times for the Executive MBA programs in the area. It allows me to give back to the community, share my knowledge, increase my network of colleagues, and connect with new thinkers. Of course, I've also found that I do get hired years later by students who remembered me.

Dana Todd of SiteLab harnesses the power of speaking gigs to build her own credibility, get her name out, and bring her a steady supply of prospects. As an interactive expert, she speaks on viral marketing, social networking sites, and hot Web trends. With her distinctive pink hair, she is truly unforgettable!

By teaching at a college or university as the lecturer for the entire course, your name gets included in the ultimate advertising vehicle: the class catalog. Often, these mailers are sent to 100,000–450,000 homes! And, each and every one has your precious name, bio, and credentials. By the way, you also collect a fee for teaching the class; it's almost like being paid to advertise!

HAL LEFKOWITZ

Hal Lefkowitz has been teaching at the University of California San Diego for years and is also part of the adjunct faculty at National University where he teaches in the MBA program. As Hal tells it, teaching keeps him up on the "state of the science," allowing him to become a more valuable speaker and consultant.

Sharing Your Information

You'll probably find that by speaking and teaching, you've assembled a boatload of valuable information. Should it go to waste? No! You can use it in so many ways to help build your reputation and reach:

- **Turn It into an Article**—As discussed in Chapter 13, you can write by-lined articles for both print and online publications.

- **Pitch a Column**—Business journals, periodicals, big portals (Yahoo!, iVillage, Slashdot, etc.,) and daily newspapers frequently need permanent contributors. Send a query letter today!

- **Create a White Paper**—If you are building your database of prospects, create a PDF of your article and offer it for free, provided Web visitors include an e-mail address.

- **Turn It into an Audio CD**—Thanks to new technology, you can easily digitally record one or all of your lectures and presto! You now have an audio course on the topic. By getting an ISBN number (see isbn.org), you can also post online at major sites such as Amazon and Barnes & Noble, providing additional exposure and even revenue.

- **Create a Video Project**—Besides the omnipresent YouTube, check out business sites such as Insight 24, Ted.org, and Helpfulvideo.com. Of course, video at your own site is also a good option. One of my favorite projects to help you with your video endeavors is *"How to Keep Your Do-It-Yourself Video From Looking Like You Did it Yourself"* by Jim Staylor.

• **Write a Book**—A very clear pathway exists between expert status and book author; you are the authority when you write the book on the topic. Self-publishing today is an affordable option. With major players such as Amazon now in the business (Book Surge, Lightning Source, Author House), you can outsource as much or as little as you like from cover design to copywriting to indexing. If you're worried about how to write a book, there are additional resources to the rescue (see Sarah Victory's CD *"How to Write a Book in 60 Days"* And Dan Poynter's book *The Self-Publishing Manual*). You might also find it helpful to record your book into a recorder and have it transcribed. And, don't forget working with a ghostwriter remains a valid option for many "authors."

• **Create an E-book**—If you don't even want to bother with self-publishing, an easier option is an e-book. If you can use Word, you can probably create an E-book. And, you can set the price, accept PayPal, and accept the revenue.

• **Break It into E-mail Segments**—You can break your lecture or speech into large chunks that become part of an on-going e-newsletter. Every week, month, or quarter, you can measure strong doses of your expertise to readers.

• **Provide Content on Your Web site**—We are in the information age. If your site explains the topic well, you can convert browsers into buyers.

• **Start a Radio Show**—Creating an Internet radio show is a relatively easy and affordable option that pays dividends. Patsi Krakoff started the *Blog Squad* as an informational resource for growing a business online, which also brings her prospects and customers daily.

MARY GOULET AND HEATHER REIDER

These two enterprising women started a radio show years ago, and because of that name recognition they were able to sign a book contract with Simon and Schuster for It's All about You: Live the Life You Crave, and land tremendous media coverage including a spot on CBS' The Early Show.

RED HOT EXAMPLE

Work the Web

You can boost your credibility online in a number of ways. If you're an avid reader, like me, you can still start writing reviews in your subject area. Business books are published by the thousands, and many of these authors are begging readers to post reviews. A simple Google search will reveal a host of resources. And, if you are already published, your reviews can be hot-linked right back to your book offered for sale!

YOUR TURN TO ACT

Start your query letter today for a print or online publication. Include your credentials, why readers would be interested, and a sample of your writing.

Explore teaching opportunities in the area, even if just as a guest lecturer. Most courses list the e-mail address of the permanent professor, making it easy to connect.

Look at the Top 25 events in your community. Go online to determine if their target market overlaps with yours; review their demographics sheet and sponsor requirements.

Go on a mission to help a charitable organization in which you are passionate. Donate in-kind, give your time or expertise, sit on the board, or help raise funds. Schedule the time and find a way to work with at least one event per year.

Chapter 17

Spread the Fire
How to Use E-mail to Extend Your Brand

Top Ways for Your E-mail to End Up in the Spam Bucket:

Use bcc (blind carbon copy). If the recipient's e-mail address is not in the "to" field, it typically is filtered as spam.

The "from" and "reply to" addresses are different. Since so much spam spoofs legitimate e-mail addresses, smart filters check for this conflict.

Use words and phrases with the following in the subject line:

- Viagra
- Online pharmacy
- Free
- Check this out!
- Past Due Account
- Re: Your Order
- Please verify your information
- Please resend your e-mail

- Information You Asked For
- Get out of debt
- Special Offer
- Online degree
- Rolex
- Work from Home
- Lowest mortgage/insurance rates
- As seen on Oprah

We all know that e-mail has forever changed the way we do business. But, we should also be looking at ways to maximize the impact of this important tool on our brand.

Setting Up Your E-mail

Once you have a domain, it's essential to set up your e-mail such as bob@bobtheplumber.com. You don't want an e-mail that ends with AOL, Yahoo, or any other company since your goal is to build your own brand name's recognition, not theirs!

Here are a few rules to remember when creating your e-mail.

- **Keep It Simple**—Try for simple first names, if possible.

- **Capture All Misspellings**—Even if you think you have a relatively simple first name, such as Barbara, you should also make sure that if customers assume you've adopted the spelling of Barbra Streisand (without the third "a"), then the e-mail will still reach you without the demon- dreaded 'mailer daemon." To this day, I remain confused about Colette Carlson; is it one l and two t's? She has all of the misspellings!

- **Keep the Same Formula for All Employees**—If your e-mail is nancy@altacopy.com, then your assistant Jane Smith would clearly be jane@altacopy.com. Get it?

- **Avoid Hyphens and Underscore**—Please let me underscore this point. We do not want underlines because all e-mails in documents revert to underlines, so we can't tell if it is there or not.

- **Always Include a Signature**—By signature, I mean the contact information at the bottom of your e-mail. It should, at minimum, include your phone number, tagline, and hot link to your Web page address. You can also attach a V-card (virtual business card), which allows recipients, especially Outlook users, to quickly add your contact information to their database.

Names and Letters Don't Mix Well

Never combine letters and numbers, as in the case of paula985873@aol.com; these are the most frequently forgotten combinations. It is the major reason why we can remember our address or our phone number, but our license plate number is extremely difficult to recall.

And, men, please promise me you'll never create an e-mail again such as "mike007" or "superbob007." I know you revere James bond, but just say no!

Also, the letter "l" and the number "1" are so similar that it's impossible to tell which is which—again leading to confusion.

WORDS of "LIZDOM"

SIMPLIFY YOUR E-MAIL

Make your e-mail address simple: liz@redfirebranding.com. If you're a small business, leave off last names. Also remember to capture all misspellings of your first name. For example, if your name is Shawn, then the names Shawn, Shaun, and Sean should all come to you so that the writer doesn't receive the dreaded "mailer demon."

It's Not E-mail All the Time

Irony and humor often don't translate well via e-mail. If you're concerned about how to write something, I urge you to pick up the phone! We have all fallen victim to thinking our tongue-in-cheek style worked, when in actuality it offended the reader. If in doubt, call!

Sending E-mail Blasts

We can all now with a click of our mouse send thousands of e-mails to our database. That's the good news; the bad news is that our prospects and customers may not want to hear from us. What are we to do?

- **Ask your database**—Allow them to decide how frequently they want to hear from you. Big retailers such as Williams-Sonoma, for example, follow this rule. Some customers receive notices weekly while others only hear from the retailer monthly.

- **Use a reliable service**—You cannot send out a mailing with your address in the subject line and "bcc" (blind carbon copies—what a throwback term!) to your list. Bcc's are often immediately put into the spam bucket. Constant Contact, Blue Hornet, and dozens of other companies all offer sophisticated tools for e-mailing.

- **Have one-click opt-out**—Perhaps you're like me and are annoyed when an unwanted e-mail states "click here to unsubscribe" only to find that it makes you retype your e-mail or change your preferences or log-in before you can do anything. Good grief! Sticking to a one-step opt-out process also allows you to remain in compliance with CAN-SPAM legislation.

- **Check out the preview pane**—Given the success of Outlook, Yahoo, and Microsoft Live offering preview panes as a default option, most recipients will receive your e-mail in this type of format. Therefore, check your e-mail to ensure that all of the important (good) stuff, including your main "call to action," can be viewed at a glance.

- **Avoid the spam bucket**—Exclamation points, words such as "free," "now," "hurry," and any reference to a pharmaceutical drug frequently land you in the spam bucket. As much as it makes me cringe as a marketer, you have to tone down this type of promotional language so that you can reach your target.

- **Track your metrics**—As Katherine Brown of e-Mail Networks notes, it makes no sense to blast an e-mail if you cannot tally the results, such as open rates. Open rates vary widely, with most companies reporting a steady decline since e-mail made its massive debut. This decline is due to an increase in spam, an increase in Internet Service Providers (ISPs) such as Gmail and Hotmail blocking images by default (image loading is how open rates are tracked), and more deletions by the subscriber. With that said, open rates are good for measuring short-term trends and comparing e-mail campaigns against each other. Therefore, you should not only be checking open rates, but click through rates (the percentage of folks who clicked on something in the e-mail that then hot-linked them over to your site), and conversion rates (the percentage of readers you converted into buyers.) Both of these are the best indicators of how your e-mail blast performed.

- **Test and test again**—The beauty of e-mail is e-mmediate! You can get your results in as little as a few hours. I remember a great test ProFlowers.com conducted; it simply split their e-mail list into two: one half received the offer of "$10 off your order of roses," and the other half received "buy roses and get the vase free." Guess which one won? (No peeking!) The free vase! Why is this information important? Because the $10-coupon costs the company $10, whereas the vase only costs the company (now operating under the E-commerce name) a mere $2.78. I also conducted a simple A/B test, as this type of marketing research is called. Everything was the same except the subject line. In every single one of your e-mail initiatives, you should try to test something: the graphics, the offer, the click through rates, etc. Your goal is to find out what works with your prospects and customers.

- **The most important list is your own**—Do not rent a list; do not borrow a list, do not tag onto someone else's list. As we discussed earlier about scanning cards and building your database, no database will ever be more important than your own.

DONNA WOLF

The newsletter by Donna Wolf, registered dietician and owner of Healthy Directions of Poway, is one of the few that I not only read, but also often archive and refer back to. Two standouts of hers were the listings of local farmers' markets and easy and healthy back-to-school snacks. Delicious!

RED HOT EXAMPLE

Creating a Great E-Zine

If you're ready to launch or improve your e-newsletter communication, remember that according to Forrester Research, eight out of ten users delete commercial e-mail without even reading it, and six out of ten say most e-mails don't offer them anything of interest. SO, how do you stand out from the pack?

- **Always use the same "from" address consistently**—We build relationships with people and brands. An e-mail from joe123@idonotknowyourcompany.com is a sure candidate for deletion. The number-one factor in determining if your e-mail gets opened is who it is from.

- **Write an intriguing subject line**—Many e-mail marketers have had tremendous success using the recipient's name as in "Liz, join me for my teleseminar?"

- **Send on a consistent schedule**—If you've agreed to write a newsletter every Monday, it must be there Monday. It cannot be a haphazard occurrence leading the recipient to exclaim, "What a surprise!" Your readers should be expecting your e-mail on a consistent basis.

ALEXANDRIA BROWN

Alexandria Brown started her business in 1998 using the Web to help other businesses boost their business. After delivering success for big-name clients such as The New York Times, Digital Books, and Scholastic Books, she started to share her Web secrets with other women through downloadable products and e-zines. Today, she is known as the E-Zine Queen, coaches hundreds of entrepreneurs each year, delivers sold-out seminars, and of course, writes her own weekly e-zine called "Highlights on Marketing and Success." Way to go Ali!

- **Play up new**—Your e-zine is a great vehicle for introducing new products, discussing new trends, talking about just-released statistics, or any item relevant to your subscriber list.

- **Offer value**—In the same vein, look for new ways to add value. It can be in the form of tips, tools, techniques, a coupon, or even a special offer.

- **Keep it short**—You are welcome to start a meaty article on *"Ten Secrets to Grow Your Business,"* but only list numbers one and two; the rest of the article hot-links over to your site.

- **Include graphics**—Include graphics, if they serve a purpose. In my newsletter, for example, I always list where I am speaking, but I also include the logos of the companies or associations that are sponsoring me. Why? Because the familiar brand logo can elicit an immediate response. I also make sure that the logos as well as the words are clickable right back to the site for more information. Recent tests have shown that clickable graphic icons that link to more details of a marketing offer draw stronger responses than links that use the text of an Internet address.

- **Make it easy to scan**—Since recipients only read 35 percent on average of an e-mail, make it easy to skim; put bullet points and headers to good use.

When to E-mail

Of course, the data here is a moving target. Once marketers figure out the best day to e-mail, it becomes the worst day because it opens the e-mail floodgates. But, there are a few rules to keep in mind.

- **Avoid right before or after a holiday**—Unless, of course, you are a retailer. E-mails on the Wednesday before Black Friday and early Friday morning have shown tremendous success in luring shoppers to spend. On the other hand, the only e-mails that work after Christmas are those screaming "after-Christmas sale." In the business-to-business arena, skip communicating with prospects until the bulk of them are back to work.

- **Days of the Week**—The best days to reach businesspeople are Tuesdays through Thursdays, 8 a.m. to 3 p.m. For consumers, aim for Friday through Sunday between 5 p.m. and 8 p.m.

YOUR TURN TO ACT

Review your business card now to see if your e-mail is easy to read, clear, has no combinations of letters and numbers, and uses the same formula for every employee.

Determine how you would use an e-zine to add value to your prospects and customers. If you are not a good writer, do not have the time or resources, and are struggling to find appropriate content, skip it. If, on the other hand, writing is second nature, and you have tons of ideas, then issue one e-zine as a test and ask for feedback. Review your open rates against the norm.

Compare your e-zine to the guidelines issue above; are you e-mailing on the right day? At the right time? Is it easy to skim?

Chapter 18

Warm Up and Follow Up
Direct Selling Secrets That Work

I love network marketing; I revere direct selling, and I adore all of the top-selling individuals in this industry. Why? Because if they are at the pinnacle of success, they have become masters of branding!

We used to call this industry Network Marketing or Multi-Level Marketing, but then marketers discovered that perhaps this name had negative connotations. So, it morphed into Direct Selling just as quickly as prunes changed into dried plums, used cars become certified pre-owned vehicles, and trash collectors became sanitation engineers.

You Are the Brand!

There are so many good companies out there selling terrific products: Usana, Arbonne, Doncaster, Send Out Cards, Silpada, Cookie Lee Jewelry, Noni, and MonaVie. The bottom-line is that these are great products that can be purchased by anyone. Your goal is to make sure buyers purchase from you!

It is your personality, your brand, and your attitude that will ultimately determine your success. If prospects see your energy and positive attitude, they become more interested in becoming part of your downstream. If they adore your follow-up, they will not simply rave about the product, they will rave about you!

Industry Overview:

A few words about the Industry:

Women dominate direct selling with almost 75 percent of all positions taken by the female gender. This statistic is great news for you if you are a woman, because women tend to develop friendships quicker, embrace new people, demonstrate empathy, and are fervent word-of-mouth promoters. Approximately 80 percent of sellers who sign up with a direct selling company stay less than one year. And, not surprisingly, it is the first 90 days that will determine whether the newcomer will become a long-term, successful member of the organization or simply disappear.

Treat Your Business as a Business

Regardless of the product you are selling, you are the business. Let me repeat: you are not a Silpada salesperson, you are the CEO of Jane Doe Enterprises, which sells Silpada, manages a team of other Silpada representatives, motivates your distributors, and helps turn dreams into reality. You must treat your business like a business and run it like a business, even if it is strictly part-time. You are actually the brand.

Since you are in direct competition with every other direct seller for the corporate brand, your challenge is to find your brand DNA—the key point of difference that sets you apart. As discussed in Chapter 1, this is the time to focus on the small items that add up to a total of a big advantage for choosing you over another sales representative.

SABRINA D'AGOSTINO

Sabrina D'Agostino has become a powerhouse in network marketing by always going the extra mile. In her YTB (Your Travel Business) career, she has earned a Sapphire Ring, indicating that she made over $100,000 in her first year of business. For her clients, she keeps meticulous notes to remember birthdays and anniversaries, and she pairs these dates with opportunities to travel. Recognizing that her distributors' success contributes to her success, she is dedicated to training, teaching, and motivating her downstream. She created hands-on training material that culminated in the publication of her book, Living Life Residually. Sabrina is cruising!

Summary of Branding Secrets

As a marketer in a relationship business, this is the time to hone those skills and activities that reward relationship building. As a result, impersonal advertising is not a good business prospect or building tool. Instead, your efforts should focus on the following "hit list" culled from this entire book that will seriously allow you to succeed:

- Distribute business cards at every opportunity.

- Master your 7-second hook.

- Create a trademarked style.

- Learn to sell benefits that emotionally connect your customers to your brand.

- Extend your reach by attending new groups or associations and by using the power of social networks online.

- Determine if certain phrases seem to resonate better with prospects and start using them to close more sales.

- Revisit the power of snail mail for thank-you cards, "thinking of you" cards, and birthday cards.

- Prepare your presentations as if a small speech: collect business cards, hold a raffle, and follow-up after the event.

- Don't forget to advertise your business with your car. Vanity license plates, magnets, and bumper stickers all spread your brand for free.

- Rediscover the phone. If you find that you use all e-mail, all the time, try designating time every week strictly for phone call follow-up.

- Record a signature voice greeting that tells callers about the benefits of working with you.

- If your corporate e-mail address is too long or convoluted, don't be afraid to use an easier one; just make sure all e-mails from all accounts feed into one "in" box.

- Explore how to set up a mood at your next event with appropriately paced music or even a signature scent.

- Find out about creating a premium to let distributor prospects and customers remember you.

- Get a permanent name tag created so that you can say goodbye to the cheap, paper ones provided at networking events. It also works to increase recall of your name.

- Having great success? Don't forget to toot your horn through the power of the press, Web, or by-lined articles.

- Sign up to receive reporters' queries so that you can seize the opportunity to get into the media.

- Tie-in your company with a relevant philanthropic cause; do well by doing good.

- Respond to e-mail "e-mmediately."

- Determine if an e-zine could work for you. You might create one for customer prospects and one with helpful and motivational ideas for your downstream.

Don't forget the golden rule of branding: every interaction counts. You want to remain consistent from encounter to encounter. Now is the time to succeed!

JUDI FINNERAN

RED HOT EXAMPLE

Networking queen Judi Finneran has built her entire career upon networking and relationships. In the first ten years of her real estate career, she sold at least seventy-five houses per year for ten years. And then, as part of Beach Body, a multi-level marketer, she has over 7,000 people in her downstream! Today, she is owner of TeamWomen, devoted to women growing their business through the power of networking. WOW!

YOUR TURN TO ACT

Create a detailed set of goals for the first 90 days. Since this is "make or break" time in direct selling, your goals must be objective and measurable. Include number of appointments, number of follow-up calls, and sales goals for the week and month.

Plan a reachable number of new groups to attend to expand your reach.

Explore LinkedIn, Twitter, and other social networking sites.

Liz Goodgold

Answers throughout the book:

CHAPTER 1
1. F
2. A
3. I
4. K
5. L
6. M
7. B
8. N
9. O
10. D
11. H
12. E
13. C
14. J
15. G

CHAPTER 2
1. D
2. F
3. B
4. E
5. C
6. I
7. H
8. A
9. G
10. J

CHAPTER 3
1. D
2. H
3. I
4. L
5. C
6. J
7. F
8. M
9. B
10. E
11. G
12. A
13. K

CHAPTER 4
1. A
2. C
3. E.
4. F
5. D
6. G
7. B

CHAPTER 5
1. D
2. G
3. B
4. E
5. A
6. F
7. C

CHAPTER 6
1. D
2. G
3. A
4. F
5. E
6. B
7. C

CHAPTER 7
1. H
2. B
3. G
4. D
5. E
6. A
7. C
8. F

CHAPTER 8
1. E
2. H
3. I
4. C
5. A
6. J
7. D
8. B
9. G
10. F

CHAPTER 9
1. H
2. B
3. K
4. L
5. J
6. C
7. A
8. E
9. F
10. D
11. G
12. I

CHAPTER 10
1. E
2. C
3. H
4. D
5. A
6. I
7. G
8. B
9. F

CHAPTER 11
1. CHANEL NO. 5
2. VANILLA
3. WOMEN
4. 2%
5. ROSE
6. CITRUS

CHAPTER 12
1. C
2. B
3. G
4. H
5. D
6. L
7. J
8. E
9. K
10. A
11. I

CHAPTER 13
1. E
2. F
3. C
4. G
5. A
6. D
7. B

CHAPTER 14
1. B
2. D
3. E
4. H
5. F
6. C
7. A
8. G

CHAPTER 15
1. C
2. B
3. D
4. G
5. F
6. A
7. H
8. E

CHAPTER 16
1. C
2. D
3. G
4. E
5. A
6. B
7. F

† indicates reference is within a *Strike the Match* or chart.

M

N

Liz Goodgold

X

X-box 134
Xerox 43, 149
xeroxcorporationsucks.com 149
xeroxstinks.com 149

Y

Yahoo! 28, 70, 196, 202, 204
Yankees 145
Yellow Tail †82, 84
You've Got Mail 21
Your Wings of Financial Security 44
YouTube 25, 65, 150, 196
YTB (Your Travel Business) 213

Z

Zegna, Ermenegildo 22
Ziegler, Zig 37
Zien, Sam 161
Ziploc 171

About the Author...

Speaker and author Liz Goodgold is a fiery redhead with over 25 years of experience in marketing and branding. In addition to this book, she also authored *DUH! Marketing: 99 Monstrous Missteps You Can Use to Learn, Laugh, and Grow Your Business.*

Liz has worked for such major clients as Quaker Oats, Univision, and Arco Oil as well as with small business owners and start-ups. Her specialized, one-on-one branding and coaching programs spark new ideas that deliver sure-fire results.

An often-quoted expert, Liz has appeared in over 500 media outlets including ABC, NBC, CBS, PBS, CNBC, CNN, The Wall Street Journal, and The New York Times.

Contact her at: Liz@RedFireBranding.com and 858-550-7000.

A Message from Happy About®

Thank you for your purchase of this Happy About book. It is available online at http://happyabout.com/redfirebranding.php or at other online and physical bookstores.

• Please contact us for quantity discounts at sales@happyabout.info

• If you want to be informed by email of upcoming Happy About® books, please email bookupdate@happyabout.info

Happy About is interested in you if you are an author who would like to submit a non-fiction book proposal or a corporation that would like to have a book written for you. Please contact us by email editorial@happyabout.info or phone (1-408-257-3000).

CPSIA information can be obtained at www.ICGtesting.com
Printed in the USA
BVOW032040220911

271839BV00004B/3/P